TEAM LEADERSHIP IN THE SOCIAL SERVICES

Edited by
John Cypher

BASW PUBLICATIONS 1982

i

Published and distributed by the British Association of Social Workers, 16 Kent Street, Birmingham B5 6RD, England.

Acknowledgements

Throughout the 1970s and into the 1980s, issues surrounding the role of team leader in the personal social services have been considered both in the literature and in various study courses. Few books, however, deal specifically with the role and functions of team leaders. Rolf Olsen's "Management in Social Services – The Team Leader's Task" was well received but it has been out of print since 1979.

The idea for a new and enlarged publication on team leaders came from BASW's former Publications Officer, Jacky Steemson, and all of the contributors to this book responded to a notice calling for material which she placed in Social Work Today. My thanks are due to Ms. Steemson for viewing a book on this topic as a necessary important addition to BASW's publications list. Without the many and magnificent contributions made by my Personal Assistant, Dominga De La Cruz, the book might not have appeared – to her secretarial skills which are well appreciated in BASW circles, she now adds expertise in sub-editing.

BASW's changing fortunes have caused some difficulties in bringing the book to publication. My special thanks are extended to the contributors, many of whom completed manuscripts by late 1981, for their understanding and forbearance in dealing with an editor subject to many other distractions.

John Cypher
May 1982
Birmingham

ISBN: 0 900102 31 4

Produced by Lapex Graphics Limited, Heswall, Wirral L60 7SE

Contents

Contributors

John Cypher, General Secretary, British Association of Social Workers.

Rosalind Lyons, Senior Social Worker, Essex Social Services.

Ann McDonald, Senior Lecturer in Social Work. ⎫
⎬ West Sussex Institute of Higher Education
Pamela Ritchie, Part Time Lecturer in Social Work. ⎭

Beryl Pain, Special Services Officer, (Planning and Evaluation) North Tyneside Social Services.

Bill Bennett, Assistant Area Officer, Hammersmith and Fulham Social Services.

Barry Barnes, Area Group Head, Camden Social Services.

John Loughran, Area Team Leader, Islington Social Services.

David Johnston, Area Officer, Warwickshire Social Services.

Colin Hardy, Deputy Area Organiser, Essex Social Services.

Stephen Nixon, Staff Tutor in Social Studies, Universities of Birmingham.

Malcolm Payne, Chief Executive, Liverpool Council for Voluntary Service.

Team Leadership in the Social Services
John Cypher

Team Leadership in context: from Seebohm to Barclay

The Seebohm report in arguing for the creation of a "social service department" (sic) drew attention to the importance of "a comprehensive area team approach".[1] It suggested the number of social workers required in the team to serve a population of 50,000 to 100,000; it pointed to the necessary major teamwork effort required in providing services and further envisaged that each area office would be under the control of "a senior professionally trained social worker with a grasp of administrative issues and wide powers of decision".[2] The area team was viewed as being well placed to engage in community development and in preventive work; here the *head of the area office* should see his function as "relating the office to the local community, as well as providing the established social services and managing its internal organisation".[3] Although teams and team work were part of the Seebohm vocabulary, interestingly the term *team leader* appears not to have been in vogue.

If the Seebohm Committee made no explicit reference by name to team leaders, by 1973, the term was evidently in use, and the role and functions raising sufficient questions for a conference to be held at the University College of North Wales, Bangor. This conference, under the title "Management in the Social Services – The Team Leader's Task" resulted in the publication of a collection of papers edited by Rolf Olsen and distributed by BASW.[4]

Although Olsen and his colleagues in North Wales saw fit to dedicate a conference to issues confronting team leaders within the personal social services, the first major book offering systematic review of the problems and prospects of organising work within social services departments, makes no reference within its index to "team leaders".[5] Closer inspection bears fruit, however, in that within the book chapter concentrating on the organisation of fieldwork, one reads:

> "Discussions with practically every department with which we have contact suggests continuing uncertainty about the supervisory role specifically at the 'team leader' level."[6]

The concerns then being voiced were converted by Brunel researchers into two fundamental questions:

1. the right if any of the supervisor to give firm instructions to a social worker, when it is the latter who is in direct contact with the client.

2. whether the prescriptive role can be contained by the supervisor along with that of an enabling role.

Taking account of opinions received from a range of staff in social services departments, Brunel researchers concluded supervisors were allowing social workers to act within delegated discretion. Although having established that supervisors were required to intervene in and direct the practice of social workers, questions were raised about their capability in relation to the social workers for whom they had responsiblity. Reflecting on the actual and potential practice competence of social workers, a scheme was proposed to distinguish managerial from supervisory relationships and locate these in appropriate post holders. Thus it was envisaged that whereas team leaders might appropriately exercise full managerial responsbility for "junior" social workers, in the case of relationships between team leaders and more experienced practitioners working relationships with less complete control elements were posited.

Issues concerning the capability of supervisory staff to undertake their task were examined further by the Birch Committee which reported in 1976.[7] It was noted that supervisory posts were often quickly reached, these staff would need support and direction in assuming new responsibilities and senior management have a responsibility to assess and make provision for the further training of junior managers. The report particularly called for the availability of advanced professional studies programmes for supervisors and managers. The increasing recognition at that time of the multi-disciplinary approach to service delivery, both within the mixed teams of staff being formed within social services departments and in the co-operative working being developed with staff of other agencies suggested that in organising training for supervision, "consideration needs to be given to the skills necessary to co-ordinating a group of staff, and to the special skills in achieving collaboration in an inter-disciplinary team where some members may have a higher status than that of the team leader". The Birch Report was certain that additional study is essential if supervisors are to appreciate their distinctive contribution to the agency and its clients.

Ilse Westheimer published her book on the practice of supervision in social work in 1977, having written it in response to requests from senior social workers and staff supervisors who sought material which would give direction and guidance on the function of supervision in social work.[8] Aware of the shortage of training provision for supervisory staff, Miss Westheimer in 1969 had played some part in the establishment of the supervision option within the further social work studies programme based at the then National Institute in Social Work Training. (In 1982 the National Institute for Social Work is still a training centre offering relevant teaching, as with short course No. 35 "the team meeting as a place for supervision".) In an unequivocal statement Westheimer asserts that staff supervision in a local authority social services department exists to ensure clients are given the best possible service and the work of the department is carried out evenly and effectively. The supervisory role is seen as involving the allocation and monitoring of resources, the allocation of work to social workers, the provision of guidance to those workers about the use of their own skills and time, and the promotion and monitoring of standards of social work practice. Furthermore, the supervisor is viewed as one who at all times must maintain a broad perspective, surveying both the work and output of the team along with a particular worker's functioning in some aspects of his practice. The complex nature then of the supervisory task and the uncomfortable position in which supervisors find themselves, sandwiched between the field and management, points up the necessity of preparation and training for such an influential role.

Identifying the supervisor's primary function as supervision, Westheimer nonetheless envisages that these staff should carry a small caseload in order to provide the means to keep in touch with the skills to be taught to supervisees. What is to be taught in supervision sessions on a continuing basis is the development of a social worker's practice competence and his management of the overall caseload.

While Westheimer was writing her book on supervision, Olive Stevenson and Phyllida Parsloe were directing a research team which produced in 1978 the report "Social Services Team; The Practitioner's View".[9] Following from that major study of a sample of social services departments at work in the mid-1970s, a number of more detailed publications have appeared, one of which is Phyllida Parsloe's examination of social services area teams.[10] Parsloe's book is described by the series editors as demonstrating how little systematic planning and analysis went into the creation of "post-Seebohm" teams with growth in a short period of time being cited as impeding the scope for planning. In these very different times where negative, nil or minor growth in services is taking place, Stevenson and Hill muse about team leaders and their teams who may now be better positioned to "consider whether their functioning gives maximum opportunity for an efficient and compassionate service". What are teams, where they have come from, current problems and future prospects are the subjects of Parsloe's consideration, although we are allowed to reach page 25 of her book before the fundamental point is raised for both members and leaders of teams, "So far I have been considering teams as if I know what they are." She observes that the assumption of a common meaning of the term serves as a barrier to an understanding of the range of possible forms of work group. Since teams of whatever kind have established themselves as an integral part of social services departments and appear likely to persist in some form, Parsloe's formulation of the following question is important for all team leaders to answer – "what kind of team is best for a particular area with a particular staff group in a particular agency?"[11]

Just as Westheimer has made a connection between the role of the staff supervisor and the quality of service given to clients, so does Parsloe in commenting that the quality of team leadership "may be the most important single influence upon the nature of the team and the quality of the service clients receive". Drawing on her earlier research with Olive Stevenson, Parsloe suggests that too many team leaders are unable however to distinguish between the model of supervision appropriate to a training situation and that required in supervising staff. By allowing social workers to raise issues of their own choosing, many team leaders were active in offering support and giving advice to team members, but as Westheimer has noted, too often in social work support has come to mean whatever the supervisee does or says is not challenged sufficiently. Parsloe takes some comfort from her belief that the use of appropriate authority is becoming now a more accepted part of the team leader's role, both by leaders themselves and team members. She also considers that on the basis of more recent contacts with team leaders, following the completion of the research with Olive Stevenson, there is better understanding in social services departments of the differences between "accountability" and "responsibility".

For Parsloe it remains important to ensure an appropriate fit between the type of team and of the leadership to which the team is subject (here both team-leading and team-type are variables). In her concluding remarks on social services area teams, she reiterates the message of her 1978 study, that the most urgent need is one of training for team leaders.

Stevenson offers in the penultimate chapter of her 1981 publication[12] a suggested model for the incorporation of specialisation in an area team including an outline of the role implications for the team leader. Within a generic team, specialist units might be formed relating to client groups (five units) and to community needs and resources (one unit). Stevenson states that this model of team organisation is definitely not one in which there is to be found "a collection of individuals with specialised case loads who do not share expertise or cross boundaries".[13] The emphasis is very much on the interaction between units within the team and it is here "that the team leader's role in co-ordination of service within the team is crucial to its effectiveness". Stevenson's expectation is that the supervision of more junior staff will shift from being a principal responsibility of the team leader to be a task taken on by the "level 3" social workers in team membership. The team leader's role therefore is viewed as particularly that of manager. The training need continues to be identified but in Stevenson's view the emphasis will be on enabling the team leader to be more prepared for staff deployment and appraisal of performance as part of the overall management of work. In this the team leader would work to ensure the specialist skills of workers were used appropriately but that in providing services, team functioning as a whole was actually generic.

In 1982 the focus continues on the role of the team leader with the Barclay Working Party report[14] adding a not altogether unexpected contribution to the debate, given the re-emphasis of Seebohm's concern to relate the area team to the local community.

In the shift towards community social work, which requires individual and team work in support of potential and existing care networks in the community, the team leader's job is viewed by Barclay as particularly crucial. Team leaders are seen as needing skills both in negotiating and acquiring resources from a variety of places and in securing a co-ordinated approach from amongst a variety of statutory and non-statutory groupings. Work allocation, staff development and co-ordination of effort will all be required of the team leader as he or she leads what will be invariably a mixed group of workers. Resulting from changes to the management structure of social services departments in which there is more substantial delegation of decision taking to team level, team leaders will need to develop skills in managing the budgets and in using the knowledge acquired by the team, when participating in agency-wide priority setting and resource allocation activities.

Robert Pinker, a Barclay Committee member, who in his dissenting note takes issue with many facets of the report casts doubt on the capacity of team leaders to do all that is required in encouraging and sustaining teams in the provision of community social work.[15] In this respect his knowledge of the post-qualifying studies sector may have led to an awareness of the deficiencies of training provision to equip team leaders for current role expectations, quite apart from the expansion in role envisaged by the Barclay majority group.

From the selection of readings mentioned so far, it will be obvious how throughout the 1970s and into the early 1980s, the importance of the team leader's role continues to be emphasised. The nature of teams and team work is changing and we may now be poised to witness a new social work in which statutory agencies and the community in its component parts, enter into a working partnership to ensure more complete and effective care. However, that there is work, and important work for team leaders to undertake, is not in doubt. This work will involve leading the team in the setting of team priorities which themselves reflect analysis of individual and community problems; the team leader will use the plan so formed in negotiating both within the department and externally to secure necessary resources. These resources in addition to the key resource of staff-skill and time may be deployed more effectively through the adoption of a scheme of workload management. It falls to the team leader to ensure co-ordination between individual team members in the promotion of team efforts but also between the team and other sources of help within the community. Although a member of the team and perhaps subject to some measure of compliance with decisions taken collectively by the team, the team leader still retains a supervisory role and he or she must clarify issues of authority and accountability. Finally there is the constant underlying theme of staff development. As part of the responsibility to ensure the effectiveness of the team's efforts, the team leader must give attention to the enlargement of individual team members' knowledge and skills, ensure co-operative relationships are formed and sustained between members, and check that individual development of team members and the development of the team as a group are proceeding in a complementary manner. In all these ways staff development must be central to the role of the team leader.

From context to content

"Employing agency", "team" and "community" are all variables which will have profound bearing on the way in which the team leader selects, presents and sustains the elements which make up the role. There is choice in the way in which the team leader functions, but this choice must be made skilfully and with a sense of timing according to the changes under way within the agency, team and community. The chapters in this book have been assembled particularly to illustrate some current issues in leading teams within the personal social services, and also to provide helpful guidance in making choices to ensure better performance in team leadership. Noting that we can no longer take for granted what is meant by the term "team" (if indeed it was ever the case), Lyons's chapter explores the nature of teams as they may be found today in the personal social services, and considers particularly the potential within different types of teams for the achievement of collaborative work.

Having been introduced to the range of team types and to a specification of the requirements for collaborative working within the team, in their chapter McDonald and Ritchie provide material which opens up the meaning of team leadership. They note the common features contained in leading teams but stress the "how" of the job may differ considerably. Their analysis leads to the conclusion that team leaders must arrive at an understanding of the nature of responsibility, accountability and decision making and of their own style in leading the team. It is communication however which they regard as so essential to an effective practice; communication with the team, with senior management, with other team leaders, and in conducting public relations. Coming next, Pain explores further the position of the team leader as middle manager, noting how the choice of leadership style may be influenced by a sense of how to minimise ambiguities in the role. In a climate where social workers are being encouraged to give attention to the outcome of their efforts, Pain sees some value in the application of the technique of management by objectives. She regards the appropriate use of this as the means of bringing together personal and organisational aims, as well as the opportunity for constructive appraisal of work being undertaken. Noting developments in patchwork, the introduction and encouragement of innovation within the team is viewed as essential for inclusion in the role of team leader, otherwise there may be increased questioning about the need for such leaders.

Bennett follows and in an examination of the expectations held by social workers of their team leaders, he sees responsibility as being at the core. He is at odds with the view of the team leader as a kind of "foreman". The large measure of direction which this implies affects adversely the commitment of team members to creativity and skill development. In the latter part of his discussion, Bennett responds to the notion of community social work as expounded by the Barclay Working Party, by commending the "team approach" to serving the neighbourhood. This team approach has profound effects on the team leader's role, with the leader seen increasingly as a resource, and one used to some degree according to team decisions. Bennett is quick to point out, however, that he is not envisaging the team leader shirking management responsibilities. The monitoring and co-ordinating of team effort and direct involvement in community development, coupled with facilitating individual team members' growth in knowledge and skill, all build in to a management task.

Barnes and Loughran also address the Barclay report's insistence on the achievement of partnership between social work and the community. The task and the challenge as they view it, reside in overcoming the approach which views communities as passive recipients of services and replacement by a full recognition of the community's own contribution in meeting needs. The team leader's task becomes one of matching community need with departmental resources in such a way that team and community either may work together or with a planned degree of independence in meeting needs.

For Johnston forward planning helps the team to begin to know the community it serves and to facilitate the sense of greater control of direction (to lead the team in setting objectives is for him the great attraction in the post of team leader). More particularly it assists the team leader both in gaining a sense of perspective which can be lost by becoming over-immersed in day to day work, and in offering a scheme to evaluate the team's and one's own performance. Using forward planning the team and its leader are better equipped to argue for a larger share of the agency's resources. A detailed account is given of how through achieving a sense of direction, a possible greater share of resources and the experience of participation in a common problem-solving exercise, effective teamwork will ensue.

Hardy is also concerned with achieving team and individual team member effectiveness through an approach based on a planning cycle within which agency priorities for a community are spelt out. He particularly addresses the issue of freeing the team member from any unproductive anxiety about taking on more work than can reasonably be handled. Hardy presents an account of the introduction of a team-based workload management system, able to respond to a total team workload and to that of the individual members forming the team. Through close examination of the time available to a worker within a specified period, leader and worker can jointly agree on the components of the workload, find the time and space to encourage developmental and non-crisis activity, and judge over or under-commitment, relative to the time available, making adjustments as necessary. Through the detailed knowledge acquired by the team leader of each worker's interests, skills and capacities, and their relationship to the needs of the area to be served, there is scope for the development of a "shared team approach".

Irrespective of how the team is organised and views its mission, the team leader will have a continuing part to play in supervision. Nixon regards supervision as a process of consultation about cases, methods of work and work performance, and he explores whether worker and leader expectations are in harmony. He reports on a research study which shows considerable discrepancy in expectation; more than half the social workers in the study are dissatisfied with supervision. Working agreements are discussed in terms of their capacity to minimise differences in expectation and so usher in greater purposefulness in supervision with beneficial consequences for the worker's approach to practice.

In ensuring that the team is committed and deployed effectively to meet community needs, inevitably the team leader is involved in staff development; as Payne observes, in a broad sense it is a constant preoccupation of teams and their leaders. It is, however, for the team, the individual member and the team leader all to identify their respective contributions to staff development. Always attention should be given to measuring how far staff development procedures are achieving the principal objective of improvement in the practice competence of team members. Payne provides numerous examples of how the processes of staff development can be utilised towards this essential outcome.

Together the contributors to this book capture the current and likely future components of the role of team leader, and in so doing identify the challenges and suggest some measures by which agencies, teams and team leaders may move towards the better provision of services to individuals and communities in need. Before proceeding it may be helpful for readers to know just a little more about the people who hold the title "team leader" within social services departments. Data supplied by the Department of Health and Social Security[16] provides information about these post-holders for the majority of English social services departments in September 1978 (six authorities provided no returns). 2,481 staff at that time held posts of team leader. This compares with a figure of 10,211 staff in social worker posts, and 1,731 employed as senior social workers. Over 7,500 of the seniors and social workers were females and 1,398 of the team leaders, males. The largest proportion of male team leaders were aged 30 to 34 (401 in number) and the same is true for female team leaders (234). Regarding qualifications, 2,301 team leaders held the Certificate of Qualification in Social Work and of this total, 1,000 were female. Slightly under 100 team leaders held no qualification in social work or social service. At that time, team leaders were leading 11,942 senior and other social workers of whom 3,591 held no social work or other social services qualification. Other social work staff in post in 1978 included 414 community workers, of which 200 were females, 1,016 trainee social workers, of whom 360 were males and 2,763 social work assistants, including 479 males.

With this bare factual outline of team leaders and selected team members, the reader is invited now to consider in greater depth issues and prospects relating to team leadership in the personal social services.

References

1. Seebohm, F., Chairman. Report of the Committee on Local Authority and Allied Personal Social Services. HMSO 1968, para 592.
2. Seebohm Report, ibid.
3. Seebohm Report, para 504.
4. Olsen, M. R., ed. Management in Social Services – the Team Leader's Task. University College of North Wales, Bangor. Occasional paper No. 1, 1974.
5. Social Services Organization Research Unit, *Social Services Departments: Developing Patterns of Work and Organization.* Heinemann, 1974.
6. Social Services Organization Research Unit, ibid., page 97.
7. Birch, R., Chairman, Manpower and Training for the Social Services. Report of the Working Party. HMSO, 1978.
8. Westheimer, I. J. *The Practice of Supervision in Social Work – A Guide for Staff Supervisors.* Ward Lock Educational, 1977.
9. Stevenson, O. and Parsloe, P., Research Directors, *Social Services Teams – The Practitioner's View.* HMSO, 1978.
10. Parsloe, P. *Social Services Area Teams.* Allen and Unwin, 1981.
11. Parsloe, P., ibid., page 53.
12. Stevenson, O., *Specialisation in Social Service Teams.* Allen and Unwin, 1981, chapter 7.
13. Stevenson, O., ibid., page 134.
14. Barclay, P., Chairman, *Social Workers: Their Role and Tasks.* Report of a Working Party. Bedford Square Press, 1982.
15. Pinker, R., Appendix. An Alternative View, in Barclay? ibid.
16. Information kindly supplied by DHSS to the author in October, 1981.

The Meaning of Team and Teamwork
Rosalind Lyons

The concept of 'team' is in frequent usage in the personal social services and in particular in social work. However, it will be seen that in practice 'team' may have very different interpretations.

In the field of sport where 'team' is even more frequently employed, a closer look at its usage may help illuminate the nature of teams in the personal social services.

Firstly, there are groups such as football teams where individuals associate together in joint action and concerted effort for a common purpose. Secondly, there are groups like tennis teams who may play together, such as in a mixed doubles game, but can also operate as individuals, but all are playing the same game and play under the auspices of the same club and are led by a single captain. Thirdly, there is the gymnastics team, where individuals each perform their own specialism independently but who, together, represent every aspect of the same sport and whose activities are co-ordinated by one captain.

So, in the personal social services there are different types of teams which can be differentiated not only by the kind of work they do but by the degree of collaboration employed. An important issue is to match the right kind of organisational structure for grouping staff to the appropriate client need. It is helpful at this stage to show diagrammatically differences in work style and in types of team. (Figure 1.)

Figure 1

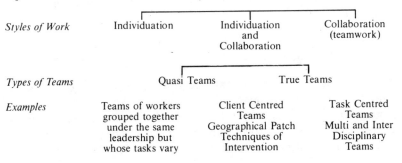

Styles of Work	Individuation	Individuation and Collaboration	Collaboration (teamwork)
Types of Teams	Quasi Teams	True Teams	
Examples	Teams of workers grouped together under the same leadership but whose tasks vary	Client Centred Teams Geographical Patch Techniques of Intervention	Task Centred Teams Multi and Inter Disciplinary Teams

In this paper the term 'work group' will be used to apply to all types of teams. Quasi teams refer to those work groups where members operate independently and true teams refer to those teams where members work collaboratively. As can be seen from the above diagram, not all true teams collaborate all the time.

In Social Services Teams: The Practitioner's View, Stevenson and Parsloe[1] suggest that social workers have failed to harness the potential of working together in true teams, teamwork, but are more frequently grouped in quasi teams which nevertheless undertake work which is specifically assigned to that team and is the team's work.

This paper will examine the nature of teams, their development, their importance to management and to the quality of service delivery. Special reference will be made to the question of the potential for and the importance of collaborative work; collaboration, not only between social workers but also between social workers and other social services personnel and between social services departments and other allied departments such as health and education.

Meeting social need is a complex enterprise and organisational structures are all important if agencies are to be effective. It is necessary therefore to be clear about the nature of the task being undertaken and to identify its component parts and the contributions each agency and individual staff member has to make. This is an area with which the social work profession at least is still grappling.

Hey and Rowbottom[2] in 1971 found that social workers lacked the ability to see their work in task terms but were mainly only able to identify isolated activities. They hypothesised that in the immediate post-Seebohm departments this might be related to a feeling of a lack of a special area of competence or an exclusive body of knowledge but still in 1978 Parsloe and Stevenson found the same thing to be true. Without clear task definition it is difficult to assess effectiveness.

"Unless you know what you are trying to do how can you begin to know whether you have done or are doing anything?" (Hey and Rowbottom.)

BASW in The Social Work Task report[3] attempted, and the NISW Working Party in undertaking a review of social workers' roles and tasks is attempting, to define the nature of social work. Hopefully this will enable the profession to clarify what the task is and how it can best be undertaken, which will have real implications for service delivery models.

Service Delivery Models

Social work, perhaps more than other professions, seems particularly susceptible to changes in fashion. But if it is to be relevant it must be sensitive to the changing needs of society and its organisations must reflect that. Often, change has taken place either in too piecemeal a manner or in too wholesale a manner, the latter rejecting the virtues of a previous system in order to embrace a new one. For example, the post-Seebohm generic social worker tended to sacrifice expertise and specialist knowledge in order to adopt the generalist approach, whereas in theory there was no reason why this could not have been retained within the generic team context.

Social and politial pressures have caused developments in one area of work to be undertaken sometimes at the expense of others. For example, the demand for improved services for abused children has sometimes meant switching resources from other areas of work such as with the mentally and physically handicapped.

An examination of job advertisements for social services over the past few years illustrates the changes in emphasis which have taken place with specialist posts gradually returning.

Sometimes changes in ideology and financial necessity work together to produce changes in service provision. At the present time the demand for alternatives to residential care for all client groups, but particularly children, has coincided with increased pressure on local authorities to make savings. Thus there is a switch in resources from residential to community care – from the provision of community homes with education to fostering and intermediate treatment.

Special local conditions will be reflected in organisational structures and the development of specialist skills. The kind of problems which might bring about local developments are a high percentage of elderly or young families or immigrants, high levels of unemployment, scattered rural or dense urban population.

Ideally structures should be based on rational service planning with the aim of matching resources to client need in an equitable and comprehensive system. The reality is that too frequently resources are inadequate, the social work profession is held in low esteem, agencies are poorly staffed and manpower planning policies are under-developed. Need is often substituted for expediency as the criteria for determining organisational structures and social workers are grouped together in order to maintain minimum levels of service rather than to optimise the meeting of client need.

13

Too often attempts to cope with organisational problems have been tackled in a piecemeal way without regard to the effects on other parts of the system. The introduction of intake teams by some agencies as a method of coping with the increased demands on the post-Seebohm departments frequently failed to take into account the effect this would have on the other parts of the organisation, yet it is impossible to alter one part of the system without it having repercussions on the others. Often the opportunity was missed to examine the whole structure to see what kinds of teams were actually now needed to meet clients need.

In addition to the factors already identified such as social and political pressures, financial implications, prevalence of problems, and bombardment rates, service delivery models must take into account, for example, the kind of community that is wanted (whether it is to be dependent or independent), the balance between reactive and proactive work, the skills and experience of the staff, and the availability of community resources. As each area will be different so the kinds of teams of workers needed will be different.

Teams can be categorised in different ways, but one way of defining them is according to how they work and the nature of their work. Thus social services teams might be categorised as follows:

(a) Task-centred Teams;
(b) Client-centred Teams;
(c) Geographical Patch Teams;
(d) Multi and Interdisciplinary Teams;
(e) Teams organised by methods of intervention.

These are not necessarily mutually exclusive. For example, it would be possible to have a multi-disciplinary team coping with the needs of the elderly – a combination of (b) and (d). These teams will be at varying points on the individuation-collaboration continuum in Figure 1.

While most work groups are likely to fall between the two extremes, it is possible that most could move with great advantage towards collaboration.

Quasi Teams

These are work groups without any clear group task and whose members rarely engage in collaboration or team work. They are individuals grouped under the same leader to whom they are accountable. It may be that there is a theoretical group task in that all the work undertaken by the team is located in the same geographical area or serving the same hospital but in practice work is undertaken in isolation and is not part of a common strategy. Some workers may in fact be members of other groups which are more significant in terms of collaborative action. For example, hospital social workers may be members of both a social work team and a multi-disciplinary team. While in theory they are accountable to the senior social worker, in practice strategies and treatment plans for clients are under the direction of a consultant. Social workers in such settings may find themselves in situations of tension as the policies and practices of the two teams they are members of may not be identical. In reality the social work team may not always operate as a true team but should be considered as a quasi team although there will be elements in its performance which are the same as true teams.

Such work groups may engage in tasks secondary to the social work activity to help bind members together into an identifiable unit, maybe by drawing attention to and accentuating the individual nature of their work which separates them from other groups.

Quasi teams may be units devised for managerial convenience or arise out of necessity where there is an insufficient number of workers to operate another scheme.

So, while the work of the team may be clearly recognised in that, for example, they are responsible for a specific number of cases, they do not engage in team work and thus the the label 'quasi' may be applied.

Client Centred Teams

These contain workers with interest in similar problems who are able to build up expertise. Many workers have a preference for working with, and skills relevant to a particular client group and this type of team enables that talent to be utilised and developed. Groupings tend to reflect the three pre-Seebohm departments – children, welfare and mental health. This method or organisation does appear to offer job satisfaction and is an easily identifiable structure to which other agencies, such as hospitals, can relate.

There is a growing trend towards a return to these kinds of formulations. They do have the advantage of allowing integration of social workers with other social service staff. For example, a team working with the elderly and physically handicapped could include home help organisers and occupational therapists. It also allows the opportunity for making closer links with the specific parts of the residential services catering for the client group.

The disadvantages of operating in this way are that such specialisation could affect flexibility in transferring staff within a department and could encourage a tendency to view cases in a narrow way in terms of the identified client with a resultant failure to tackle other problems in the client system. New workers would need to be specially catered for through planned transfers in order for them to have a real opportunity to discover their interests.

Geographical Patches

The patch system also offers the opportunity for workers to collaborate rather than work as individuals. There is increased possibility of building good working relationships with other agencies, including voluntary workers, and of becoming absorbed into a network of communications which should provide an early warning system for potential problems. It should enable the development of preventive work, with social workers utilising an alternative pool of resources outside their own organisation.

The Unitary method developed by Pincus and Minahan[4] and Goldstein[5] in the United States, and Specht and Vickery[6] in Britain, could be most useful here. This is a systems analysis approach which enables the worker to view the client in his total environment and to select which sub-systems are appropriate for intervention. This could include the school, neighbourhood, church or family.

In the present economic climate, communities will consistently need to be encouraged to find their own ways of coping, with social workers acting as enablers and facilitators while others implement action. But in teams where there is a rapid turnover of staff this method of operation is difficult, because it requires long term commitment to an area and the necessary links are frequently forged through personal contact rather than strictly adhering to agency and role expectations. It is most likely to be effective in areas of dense population rather than scattered rural communities.

Multi and Interdisciplinary Teams

One of the shifts which has taken place in social work since Seebohm is the move away from the clinical (one to one) mode of social work towards working with the whole client system. This involves using a far more extensive range of resources than is at the disposal of one single social worker and for that matter one individual agency.

As Peter Leonard, in his paper Policies and Priorities[7] points out, in any given local authority social services department fieldwork staff only account for 20% of the staff. Field social workers are working alongside residential staff, day care staff, home helps, occupational therapists, just to name a few.

While these can be formed into teams there are real difficulties presented by the prevalence of hierarchical levels where most relationships are conducted in a rigid, vertical superior/subordinate manner. In seeking to create team-work amongst these staff groups clear boundaries would need to be defined and it may be necessary to differentiate between supervisory and managerial roles. However, this kind of arrangement offers real potential in providing a comprehensive and integrated service to clients. In many social services departments it may be that insufficient status has been given to non-fieldwork staff, and the resulting denial of complementary or alternative ways of using staff in residential and day care settings has hampered the development of an effective service.

The concept of 'team' as a group of workers engaged in a common task could extend beyond the boundaries of the agency to embrace health departments, housing, education, etc. One example of such collaboration is where emergency mental health assessment teams have been set up consisting of a psychiatrist, community psychiatric nurse and social worker. However, the problem of accountability across agency boundaries is still largely unresolved and impairs attempts to work together.

Teams organised according to Techniques of Intervention

These are teams whose organisation is based upon the method of intervention employed. Some task centred teams could also be included in this category, e.g. intake teams whose main methods of working are assessment, crisis intervention and short term contractual work.

Organisation along these lines appears to be little used outside specialist agencies and intake teams but appears to offer considerable advantages to post-Seebohm departments. It provides the possibility of specialisation, and the attendent job satisfaction so desired by social workers, by emphasising practice skills. Recent research has shown[8] that the development of alternatives to 'casework' has been slow. Although social workers recognised the need for and were interested in group and community work, lack of time and training has inhibited the practice of these areas of work. One might envisage a social work agency having teams which undertook the following:

(a) Intake team whose task it was to identify problems and refer on to the team who had the most appropriate skills and resources,

(b) Service provision team which provided access to resources and services such as delivery of aids for P.H., homefinding (Part III, adoption, fostering, hostel placements) welfare rights;

(c) Casework team who specialised in counselling individuals where individualised relationships are particularly important in helping clients with their problems,

(d) Group work and community work team whose emphasis would be working with the individual within the context of his environment. This would mean using family therapy, group work, liaising and co-ordinating skills.

In practice a special sub-team might need to be formed to collaborate on working with a particular client's problems requiring individual and group approaches.

There has been a tendency for social workers to try to tackle single handed and simultaneously all the problems a client presents. This has frequently resulted in confusion for the client and pressure for the worker. Breaking down client need into its component parts, converting into tasks, and identifying the skills needed to tackle these problems makes them more amenable to change. Providing the workers do co-operate together actively as a team this approach can be advantageous especially in high risk, high stress cases.

Of course a high level of trust and communication must exist between all parties and the client may be overwhelmed by having to cope with 'too many' workers.

Task Centred Teams

Task centred teams are work groups where all team members are engaged on the same kind of work which is specific with an end point, which requires a comprehensive programme of activity in order to attain it, and which has in it implicitly, if not explicity, a time scale[9]. Usually a high degree of collaboration is required from members.

An Intake Team is a good example of this. All members are engaged in the same task, namely receiving and assessing all new work referred to the department. The work is clearly defined with a start and finish.

It requires workers to reveal themselves and their methods of working in a way in which quasi members are unused to. The group experience is likely to be intense because workers are attempting to achieve consistent response to referrals.

Teams which have a clear purpose and identity need to be aware of their role within an agency or there is a danger of alienation and elitism. They are likely to experience problems of recruitment when staff changes occur, and

18

because of the specialised nature of the work must be prepared to train new members.

Task centred teams usually have clearly identifiable aims and therefore it is easier to devise techniques for evaluating the effectiveness of the performance. Intake teams, for example, have made indices of effectiveness such as decrease in re-referral rate, increased speed of response, etc.

The team as a unit of management

Any large organisation needs to subdivide itself in order to maintain control of its members and the social work agency is no exception. The size of the unit is important. Unlike manufacturing industry where there is a clearly identifiable product, the output of a social work agency is far less tangible and the process of production correspondingly complex and ill defined.

The optimum sized work group will depend on the nature of that group and the quantity and type of work it is undertaking. Where collaborative working is necessary between group members – the true team – group dynamics will become significant and the size of group should ideally reflect the accepted face to face group norm of approximately six to eight members. Larger units may be possible where individuation is more important. Size will also be determined by the capacity of the leader to exercise effective control over the group and the degree of supervision which is required.

The team leader is the grass roots worker's link with management and the wider organisation. The team leader has the task of conveying to the team changes in policy and of translating policy into day to day practice. Management will expect him to ensure its implementation. In return the responsibility of channelling social workers' ideas and dissatisfactions through the management structure lies with the team leader.

The team leader is also responsible for the quality of the work undertaken by his staff. Although the concept of a minimum level of performance is a difficult one to apply to social work practice, yet the team leader's duty to the organisation and to the client population is to monitor the level of service being offered and to ensure that no client or need is neglected and that appropriate resources are made available. The agency will be particularly concerned with the consistency of response as this is how credibility is maintained in the community. Whilst social work intervention is largely based on person to person responses, social workers should still be seen to be operating within a broad political, moral and social framework. One of the team leader's duties is to be continually questioning this framework and seeing where re-definition or modification or refinement of practice are needed. Agency policy must be dynamic and capable of responding to new situations.

The team leader will have a number of methods of control available to him. Amongst these, the team meeting is an important forum for discussion and development; it enables him to gauge the concerns of the group and the extent to which individual members may be deviating from the norms. Group pressure may be exerted to encourage the deviant member to reappraise his situation. Supervision sessions allow the exploration of the social work process, and an analysis of where social worker and client have reached in the tackling of a problem. Work allocation is also an important measure of control for it allows the matching of client problems with social work skills and interest. Team leaders can use it as a valve to put on or take off pressure, to broaden experience or to encourage specialism. Where team leaders are undertaking this function they need to exercise care and responsibility for not only are they controlling the service offered to the client but they are also shaping the course of individual social workers' careers, and must be mindful of their professional development.

Evalution of workers allows the individual and team leader to assess the progress of the worker's development and to examine the worker's relationship to the organisation.

Team leaders will be unable to deny the extent to which they are accountable to the wider organisation for the performance of their teams. Where standards of performance are unacceptable and there is a failure to initiate change by the preceding methods the team leader must look to the hierarchy to impose sanctions. This may lead him into confrontation not only with the social worker but also the trades unions.

The Team as the Primary Group
Just as large hierarchical organisations exercise control by division into smaller units, so, in turn, workers in large structures can only relate to that organisation if they are part of a small face to face group.

The need for this among social workers, particularly in quasi teams, is probablly much greater than among other workers. Being a social worker can be a lonely occupation, carrying with it a high level of responsibility and stress which goes largely unrewarded in terms of recognition, status and salary.

A well integrated and functioning work group can provide its members with the support, encouragement and understanding they need to do the job. Given a formal structure, an identifiable group sitting in physical proximity to each other, most of this will take place at the informal level. The sharing of experiences of perhaps a difficult interview, will produce examples of comparable situations from other team members who will describe how they have dealt with a similar problem – effectively or ineffectively. It provides the opportunity to relax – a haven. Humour has an important function in social work; it allows social workers to reduce stressful situations to a tolerable level. It is a real way of coping with the burden of pain and distress which is heaped upon the worker's shoulders. If team members are to nurture each other in this way there must be a high level of trust between them. In the quasi team setting, workers only infrequently have the opportunity of seeing each other at work, so the sharing of common experiences is an important developmental as well as caring forum.

For students, trainees and new entrants into social work, a well functioning team can be a real school of learning. It provides the opportunity to engage in dialogue with informed workers, and to allay fears or confirm ideas. The overheard telephone call can provide an object lesson in alternative strategies. From this group of people the new entrant will absorb the flavour of social work which may have a lasting influence on his own practice. The team leader can be greatly assisted in his task of directing and motivating new workers by team members sharing their skills and enthusiasms.

Formation of the team, its identity and ethos

Composition and membership of teams is important and must be related to the identified task. Team membership can be self-selected, management determined or negotiated. The more clearly defined the team task is and the more collaboration is sought, the more crucial appropriate membership and leadership will be. Careful selection is necessary for maximum effectiveness. Negotiated membership is likely to prove most satisfactory when possible but in order to ensure there are staff to do the job, this may not always be possible.

Newly forming teams are often in an advantageous position of being able to identify their aims and to devise a framework of operation. If actual team members participate in this exercise their commitment to its ideals is likely to be strong. Where there is a clearly articulated frame of reference and operative model, it is easier for social workers to see what will be required of them, and to assess whether or not their skills can be utilised in that setting.

True teams will need to consider the following when selecting new members; balance of experienced and inexperienced staff; formation of a group of workers whose skills complement each other; commitment to the declared philosophy; ability to accept the position of the team leader. In addition to the professional considerations, interpersonal factors cannot be ignored either. If the operation of the group demands interdependence of its members then the compatibility of personalities of these members is an important issue. For professional and interpersonal reasons, balance of age and sex of group members will also be significant. Certain team tasks will require special characteristics of members.

This points to the need to employ techniques of personnel selection in general usage in industry if one is to fit the right person to the job. Job descriptions and personnel specifications, could be used to advantage far more frequently than at present.

Once the formal structure of a team has been determined, the informal processes will take over in order to weld an identifiable working unit. Leadership style will determine the processes to some extent and an individual's personal style will have a very strong influence.[10] If a group of workers is to work realistically together then the credibility of the leader is vital. It seems that workers are more likely to allow a worker to lead with whom they are in sympathy and for whom they feel respect. This suggests a higher degree of participative management than many agencies enjoy. Social work is labour intensive. The tools are the skills and personality embodied in each social worker and in order for them to be most effective the working environment must be right. If it is not, one can expect a high turnover of staff, sickness or underfunctioning workers, and therefore immediate deterioration to the service.

In order to develop, teams must be dynamic and any leader must encourage the group to grow and explore together ways of working. Through debate and shared experiences teams will develop methods of operating that are their own. Each team will develop its own ethos and expectations. These characteristics will distinguish them from other teams and will reflect the degree of cohesiveness of the group. This sense of belonging must be a healthy growing experience and not a stultifying over-protective one. The image of the team may or may not be entirely related to professional performance or attitudes. The kind of labels which outsiders may use to identify groups can be many and varied – experts, professionals, amateurs, fun lovers, innovators, stick-in-the-muds. The names given to teams are important.

Each work group is likely to have its 'rules of membership' and these may or may not be related to task, responsibility for certain kinds of cases, level of commitment to the team meetings, who makes the coffee, who sits where, who has what quality of equipment, who plans social activities. 'Rules' are important for the smooth running of the group and useful, unless obsessional and unbreakable. Some linger on even when group members change and are important in giving continuity in an otherwise highly fluid situation.

Group Dynamics

The previous section introduced the topic of the importance of interpersonal interaction to team functioning. The nearer one wishes to move towards collaboration along the individuation/collaboration continuum the more important group dynamics will be.

Leadership styles and personalities vary and these in combination have an important impact on the functioning of teams. Stevenson and Parsloe[11] suggest that team members welcomed directiveness from their leader and were seeking more constructive criticism and control than many were receiving.

Leadership style must be appropriate to meet the needs of the team members and to enable the completion of the team task. Each type of work group will demand different skills of its leader. Groups with diverse tasks cannot expect team leaders to have intimate knowledge of every aspect of the work they cover, and there should be an expectation of sharing knowledge and expertise within the team and across team boundaries.

It will be the leader's responsibility to identify the roles of the group members and to foster the positive characteristics of each worker, and to encourage their utilisation for the benefit of the whole group. He must weld a cohesive group from the mixture of personalities and roles.

Even the apparently negative roles played by some members can be functional, for example: critic, pessimist, cynic. However, it must be recognised that there may be times when an individual is unable to accommodate the philosophy of the group and whose differences are so acute that the effective functioning of the group is threatened. Steps must then be taken to bring about changes in team membership.

Social workers' seating arrangements can have important implications for team performance. Some workers choose to face their desks away from other group members, choosing separation rather than intimacy. The dominant member of the group may enhance his or her position by choosing a strategic situation in the room. Some may become territory conscious and attempt to control their working environment by gathering books or equipment around them, acquiring specific items of furniture, personalising their environment by the introduction of photographs, ornaments or posters. Individuals and groups will have different tolerance levels of impingement on their territories and interpersonal relationships will be affected accordingly.

These apparently trivial matters will have an important bearing on the harmony or otherwise of team relationships. It is important that team members should feel physically at ease with each other if they are to benefit from the supportive environment.

Team Maintenance and Team Work

Effort is needed by all team members to ensure the cohesiveness of the group. In order to maintain this the team may need to engage in activities which do not directly further the team's tasks but whose main function is the perpetuation of the group's life – team social activities are an example of this.

Team meetings provide the rare opportunity for groups to get together to discuss topics of common interest, to plan future activities, etc. There group members tasks will be identified, and the involvement of supporting clerical, technical and administrative staff will be important for the smooth and productive operation of the team. Clerical staff who are alienated from the staff they support often lose sight of the task and the satisfaction in their job.

Frequently the pressures of a busy office limits the time allocated to team meetings. Team retreats or study days provide the opportunity for a more extended experience of team belonging. They can serve many purposes – time for a refreshment and reassessment in a related setting, a forum for examining a theme of general interest, a structure for improving relationships and exchanging ideas so providing a firm basis for teamwork.

A team approach gives the client access to a wider variety of skills and resources than are likely to be invested in one worker. While on the whole it may be easier for the client to relate to one worker, there are occasions when tasks are identified by client and social worker which that worker cannot achieve himself, or without the aid of a second person. Marital and family therapy are both examples of areas of work which lend themselves to the collaboration of two workers. A social worker encountering problems in these areas may need to enlist the help of a co-worker. Intermediate treatment may be another area where social workers wish to share cases. The intermediate treatment officer might concentrate on working with the young person while the social worker continues work with the family.

In any group situation more than one worker is needed either in observer or co-worker role. Social workers who choose this method of intervention may make good use of resources by jointly working with a group of clients in need of a similar experience.

Group supervision offers the opportunity for team members to share their skills and learn from one another. There can be accountability difficulties in this method of operation but it gives social workers access to a rich source of ideas. As the social work task increases in complexity, the need for social workers to consult with workers in addition to their team leader increases. Not only are skills and techniques shared but pressure too. Team members become more aware of the problems they are mutually coping with and can share the burden. In addition, the social worker recognises responsibility to his peers for his performance and not just to his team leader.

The team can provide the main forum for professional development. In hard economic times when training is likely to be rationed, social workers will need to draw on each other's experience rather than looking outside. Teams can take time out to discuss a case, or a method of intervention, or course experiences, in a constructive and supportive environment.

Work allocation is a task which team members can undertake together although, as has been pointed out[12], there is a tendency for the less vocal and insistent social workers to find themselves accepting too high a proportion of the work. However, it can provide the opportunity for examining theoretical frameworks and alternative methods of working. It also allows teams to gain overall knowledge of client need which may in turn result in the identification of unmet need. Team work of this kind also has a team maintenance outcome as working together on a common task unites groups.

Teams, through meetings, also have the opportunity of uncovering issues either internal or external to their organisation over which they may have a concensus of opinion. They may join together to exert influence in the form of a pressure group to bring about change in their own organisation or in the community. In local government departments direct action may be difficult and discouraged, but used at the right time can be effective.

Teamwork, however, may have the undesirable effect of alienating its members from the hierarchy or from other teams in the structure. Vertical and horizontal communication channels are vital if the service is to develop. Too often groups operate in isolation and do not share with each other the knowledge or skills they have gained.

Team Evaluation and Monitoring

One of the most important tasks a team has to undertake is to evaluate and critically examine it philosophies, performance and effectiveness. No group of workers can afford to be complacent – it must be willing to respond to change and develop new expertise to meet that change.

They must also test out their findings with other teams, especially where team interdependence exists. For example, intake teams and long term teams need to assess each other's performance. Teams must be also be prepared to seek the views of the community being served – other agencies, voluntary workers, etc., and finally and more difficult, the social worker must seek to respond to the comments of the consumer. While it will be difficult for teams to undertake extensive surveys into what clients think of the service, there are a number of ways in which the client's views can be taken into account. Social workers undertaking contractual work with clients have a ready means of evaluation built into the system, for at the conclusion of the contractual period they can arrange to spend a session reviewing with the client the achievements of the service and the applicability of the methods used.

In group situations where open and frank discussions are encouraged the ideal opportunity also exists for encouraging clients to comment on the service they are receiving, and for the group leaders to respond accordingly.

It is important that agencies develop adequate grievance procedures which gives clients a formal channel through which to express dissatisfaction of the service being offered to them and a right to a response. Social workers and team leaders must be sensitive to clients' requests, for example, to a change of worker or method of working. Including clients in plans being made for them or their families must increase client motivation and commitment to the social work process. The inclusion of children in their reviews, and clients in their own case conferences, allows both workers and clients to be explicit about aims and objectives and increases the client's control over his situation.

Social workers are beginning to move into the more difficult area of self-examination of effectiveness. Intermediate treatment specialists are developing criteria for assessing personal development of clients in a more formal way. This is still a difficult area but as social workers begin to articulate their aims and objectives more specifically it will become more possible to determine changes in client behaviour.

The introduction of casework management schemes which encourage social workers to express the purpose of their work in clearly defined objectives, allows the possibility of examining how these are achieved, and how successful an approach can be. Increased job satisfaction is a by-product of this as social workers can be aided towards more realistic expectations of the work they do with clients, and map developments and changes.

Conclusions

This paper has attempted to examine the nature of teams and their development and has suggested that more attention needs to be given to collaboration rather than individuation. Resources are being used inefficiently and a dilution of service is occurring because social workers are attempting to be all things to all men. A team approach to the social work task can provide the worker with increased job satisfaction and enable him to develop his skills. It is more likely to satisfy the demands of management with regard to efficiency and standards of service. Teams must always be engaged in the task of self-examination so that strategies can be improved upon and unmet need recognised.

In conclusion it might be helpful to consider what the characteristics of a team pursuing collaborative working might be:

1. Existence of a common and indentifiable purpose.

2. Specific aims and objectives.

3. Negotiated selection of team members, including leader and both in and out transfer.

4. Team leader who facilitates achievement of aims and objects and liaises with the wider organisation on team's behalf.

5. Co-operation and collaboration between members.

6. Interdependence between team members based on common aims and trust built through working relationships and shared tasks.

7. Complementary roles and functions of members.

8. Identifiable strategy for achieving aims and objectives.

9. Criteria for measuring effectiveness.

10. Evaluation and monitoring of performance and strategy.

As it has been seen the degree of collaboration which teams achieve is largely dependent on their structure. Social work agencies might profitably examine these structures with a view to making the best use of staff skills.

References

1. Stevenson, O. and Parsloe, P. *Social Service Teams: The Practitioner's View*. HMSO, 1979.
2. Hey, A. and Rowbottom, R. "Task and Supervision in Area Social Work", reprinted in *Welfare in Action*. Open University 1977.
3. Report of a BASW Working Party. *The Social Work Task*. 1977.
4. Pincus, A. and Minahan, A. *Social Work Practice, Model and Model*. Hasca. Illinois. Peacock, 1973.
5. Goldstein, H. *Social Work Practice, a Unitary Approach*. Columbia, University of South Carolina Press, 1973.
6. Specht, H. and Vickery, A. *Integrating Social Work Methods*. Allen and Unwin, 1977.
7. Leonard, P. *Policies and Priorities. The Role of the Team Leader in Management in Social Services, The Team Leader's Task*. Ed. by R. Olsen. University College of North Wales, Bangor Occasional Papers, 1974.
8. Stevenson and Parsloe, *op. cit.*
9. Hey and Rowbottom, op. cit.
10. Stevenson and Parsloe.
11. *Ibid.*
12. *Ibid.*

"The standardised worker with interchangeable parts"

Ann MacDonald and Pamela Ritchie

A discussion of the task of the Team Leader as a Middle Manager in non-residential social work.

> "I tell you, sir, the only safeguard of order and discipline in the modern world is a standardised worker with interchangeable parts. That would solve the entire problem of management".
>
> Jean Giraudoux, The Madwoman of Chaillot.

Roles and relationships – "the interchangeable parts"

Implicit in the position of the middle manager is the necessity to relate to those immediately above and those immediately below him in the hierarchy. For the team leader in a social services department this entails relating, on the one hand, to those who are clearly managers, and on the other, to professional workers engaged in direct work with clients. The possibility of conflict arises from the fact that the orientation of area manager and social worker are inevitably different. The area manager's function is to organise the provision of service to a geographical area. This includes allocating limited resources, priority setting, internal organisation of the area and a public relations job. On the other hand the social worker is concerned with individual clients or families, a small neighbourhood patch or a particular client group – which is only one part of the total workload of the area office.

The team leader must understand the differences between the roles and functions of the area manager and of the team of social workers, and must accept both as legitimate. He must then accept that these differences will lead to conflict over certain issues but that without such conflict the work of the area team might well become sterile. The problem for the team leader is that he frequently finds himself in the middle of the conflict, attacked from above and below and needs therefore to be clear about his own role and responsibilities as a member of the area team.

For the first time in his social work career the team leader may find himself in the position of being a boss as well as a worker. He is a worker, directly accountable to his area manager, he is a boss responsible for the management and supervision of his team. In addition to these two roles, he is a member of a peer group of team leaders, both in his area team, and in his authority as a whole.

The team leader must therefore be a man of 'interchangeable parts' in the sense that he needs flexibility in his relationships with those around him in his agency. However, this must not become an excuse for lack of continuity in attitude and practice.

"A standardised worker" – a definition of the task?

From authority to authority and even from area to area within the same authority, the role of the team leader can be very different even when it is acknowledged that the primary function is one of staff management. Few authority, the role of the team leader can be very different even when it is do so in rigid terms, for surely flexibility is essential to what may be the most difficult job in the department.

Our experience in working with team leaders asked to define for themselves the priority tasks within their diverse role, is that no two team leaders see their job in the same way. The differences seem to relate to 5 major factors:

(i) the way the area manager defines their task;
(ii) the way the team leader defines the task for himself;
(iii) the needs of the area;
(iv) the differing qualities of the individual workers for whom he is responsible;
(v) the way the team functions as a group.

Although team leaders may interpret the 'how' of their job very differently, there are common elements in defining the task. Team leaders are involved in supervising the work of social workers and others at a variety of levels. This includes allocation of work to the team and supervising that work until it is brought to a satisfactory conclusion (client or service oriented). He is concerned with the development of his team members and evaluating their performance in relation to this (worker oriented). He is also involved, to a greater or lesser extent, in administration, public relations and policy making (authority oriented).

One step furtherback from defining tasks is the problem of goal setting. While goals may be very different from one situation to another, there exist some common guidelines which can be identified. These are:

(1) Goals need to be clearly defined, attainable and able to be assessed in

30

concrete terms with evaluation of method as well as results.

(2) Goals for the community, team and agency need to be in harmony with one another.

(3) There needs to be a match between the aims and philosophy of the area and the capacity of those individuals within the team to meet these aims.

Within the framework of goals, tasks and methods outlined above it becomes essential that the individual team leader is particularly clear about such issues as:

(a) responsibility and accountability
(b) decision making
(c) his own leadership style, including strengths and weaknesses within the role.

(a) *responsibility and accountability*

For the team leader responsibility and accountability flow in two major directions – to his area manager above, and to his team.

In respect of the area manager the team leader needs to have defined the area of, and limits to the range of his duties. This needs to be made explicit so that both know exactly what the team leader can be held accountable for. In relation to this it is imperative that the area manager is clear about the standard at which he expects the job to be carried out. It may be convenient for some team leaders wishing to opt out of certain duties not to have the task too clearly defined. However this may rebound when an issue arises which raises the question of their accountability.

With regard to his team the team leader must establish the precise tasks, duties and responsibilities of each individual member. He must convey these to them together with his expectations of their level of performance, so that there is mutual understanding. There is also a place for ensuring that the team as a whole is aware of each others' areas of expertise and interests so that each knows to whom they can look for support and help as issues arise. However, there will be areas of personal performance that remain confidential between the team member and team leader. The need to be explicit is apparent in issues such as case recording where individual workers may have very different ideas on both the quality and content of case records.

He must also make clear to each team member, to the team as a whole, and indeed to the area, what his own responsibilities are. This may not be easy when contentious issues such as professional autonomy versus supervised

31

practice still need to be thought through in many authorities. This particular subject is brought to the forefront again with the recent restructuring of social work staff levels, arising from the 1979 salary settlement.

When workers are clear about their responsibilities, they can be called to account. For example, if the team leader has carried out all possible managerial and supervisory duties in relation to a team member who still has not functioned in a satisfactory manner, then that team member can be held accountable for the quality of his work. On the other hand if a team leader has failed to give proper supervision, he can be called to account.

(b) *decision making*

The team leader needs to be clear as to who makes which decisions. This includes which decisions are appropriately and legitimately his to make. This may differ from area to area within the same authority. In working with team leaders we have found that the kind of decisions they are involved in include:

(1) Day-to-day management and supervision of the team.
(2) Allocation of work.
(3) Casework decisions.
(4) Decisions as to how to implement departmental policy at local level.
(5) What information it is important to pass on to the area manager or elsewhere.
(6) The allocation and management of the team leader's own time within the limits set by other priorities.
(7) Some allocation of resources.
(8) Specific tasks delegated by area manager.

Team leaders are generally clear that these functions are an appropriate part of their role and can be frustrated when these are not seen to be so by their Area Manager.

Decisions made elsewhere seem to include:

(a) Made by higher management:

(1) Political decisions.
(2) Allocation of budget and priority setting.
(3) Departmental policy on broad issues.

(b) Made by fieldworkers:

(1) Day to day management of time.

32

(2) Priority setting within caseload.

(3) Casework decisions.

The areas in which there seems to be most difference in the decision making power of the team leader is the allocation of resources, with some team leaders able to spend up to £50 and more per annum per family on preventive work with children without higher authorisation, whereas in a neighbouring authority, only the area manager can sanction the spending of any money.

Implicit in the above is the fact that the team leader needs to be a person with skill in decision making. Often individual issues are not as clear cut as suggested above, or decisions have to be made at a time of stress. This calls for the ability to look at all sides of an issue clearly and speedily, to reach a conclusion and to convey the decision to those affected. The team leader may then need to stand by and justify his decision at a later date.

A common area of difficulty arises when team leaders are forced into making decisions which are not appropriately theirs to make. An example of this is 'held cases' – cases that cannot be allocated due to shortage of staff. Departmental policy may say that all cases should either be allocated or closed, but if, at a local level, there are 'statutory' cases, but no staff to whom to allocate them, it is often the team leader who has to take the decision to 'sit on' these cases for the time being.

Another argument here may be that the team leader should take on the cases himself. This raises the wider issue as to whether the team leader needs to spend his full time on his management role. It is impossible to generalise. As staff become more qualified and experienced the team leader may have spare time. It may be appropriate for him to fill this by taking on a caseload, with the inherent dangers of conflict between needs of client and team.

(c) *his own strengths and weaknesses within the role*

The professional social worker knows about self awareness in relation to his work with clients. The team leader needs to continue with and expand this area of self knowledge in relation to his new role. He needs to make a realistic assessment of his abilities and the strengths he brings to the job. He needs to recognise the limits of his knowledge and skills in order to seek help with areas of weakness. Only thus can he develop in the role. Seeking help as a team leader may be difficult if he sees doing so as a sign of failure, or if he feels the team may lose confidence in him. It can also be difficult if he has no regular supervision from his area manager in which some of these issues mentioned above can be discussed. From our work with team leaders it would seem that few have systematic opportunities for discussing their own professional development and many have little idea of their area manager's opinion of their functioning.

There cannot be any such thing as a 'standardised worker' image for the local authority team leader with the diversity of roles and functions implicit in the job. It is, however, possible to identify some common tasks, although it will not be possible to define the methodology for carrying out these tasks. It may well be possible to identify some common themes for goal setting while it is clearly not possible to identify common goals. What is essential is that the team leader works out his role, to the extent that he is clear about his tasks and function and does not respond automatically to every demand made on him to change his approach from those above or below him in the hierarchy.

Communication

The link between the definition of the team leader's role as middle manager as given above and effective practice is the ability to communicate successfully.

Successful communication is not as simple as it may appear and this is borne out by the frequency with which staff at various levels in social services departments make statements such as "we didn't know what was going on", "nobody tells us anything" and "why aren't we ever consulted about issues which affect the way we work".

Successful communication could be defined as having taken place when the message firstly has been clearly and concisely given and secondly has been assimilated and understood. What often happens is that the communicator feels that he has clearly and concisely imparted the information but fails to check that those receiving the message have understood its contents and considered its implications for their own practice. On the other hand the message communicated can be ambiguous. Consequently, the receiver interprets it differently from the way it was intended.

(a) *Changing structure of area teams*

Within area teams communication can often be clouded by a number of factors. A typical example is the introduction into the area of professionals other than social workers, for example, occupational therapists and home help organisers. Often problems arise because the relationship between the team leader and the other professional is not clearly defined. Is he a direct line manager in relation to these staff members in the same way as he is to social

34

work staff? Perhaps he just has a general 'looking after' function? Perhaps responsibility is split between the team leader and some other person in the department who has the same professional expertise as the worker in question? Whatever pattern is wanted by the authority is frequently not and perhaps cannot be, made explicit which leaves room for all kinds of confusion.

A similar problem arises when senior practitioners are responsible, as part of their role, for the supervision of other staff in the team, such as unqualified social workers, social work assistants, students or volunteers. Does the team leader communicate solely through the senior practitioner? Is the senior practitioner directly responsible to the team leader and is he accountable for the work of those he supervises or does the team leader have overall responsibility for everyone in his team? Although the team leader's style of management can ease the path, unless these issues have been clearly thought through communication for both the team leader and the senior practitioner is hazardous.

(b) *Lack of uniformity in the role of the area manager and the team leader*

We have already referred to the varying roles of team leaders. The same can be said for area managers. Indeed in our experience, these two roles differ from area to area within the same authority never mind authority to authority. However even within an area, an area manager may be communicating different expectations to each of his team leaders. This will probably relate not only to the various tasks that have to be shared between them, but also to their level of competence and expertise. An area manager may well expect one team leader to perform 'better' than another and will gear communication accordingly. The implications of this for the team leader relate to his being able to make sense of these differences in communication and from there to carve out a role for himself that is acceptable to his colleagues.

With the growth of community based teams, geographically separate from the main area office, the team leader's role can again vary as he often has to take on many of the functions of the area manager. Both need to be clear about the limits of his responsibilities and in this situation communication is complicated by physical distance.

Communication – what to communicate, to whom, and how?

(a) *Communication Upwards*

The area manager is at least two levels away in managerial terms from basic grade workers and because of this these workers may not always be clear about his role and function. The result of this may be that correct and appropriate information is not passed upwards. The team leader is nearer to the basic grade workers and from their point of view is more likely to understand their feelings about problem areas and issues of importance. The team leader's task is therefore to listen, sift and interpret information and feelings on the ground level and to pass what is relevant up to the area manager together with his own thoughts. This should enable the area manager to piece together a true picture of area needs and team functioning and therefore to respond to those needs.

But when do team leaders communicate this information upwards? Do they have formal supervision sessions or regular meetings at which this can take place? Often, communication between area managers and team leaders is poor because there is no set time to communicate about general issues. Area meetings provide one venue for communication but seldom is it possible to present a whole picture at such meetings.

The result may be that the area manager has a very piecemeal and inaccurate picture of area functioning based on feelings and presumptions rather than hard data.

(b) *Communication Downwards*

One of the issues involved in communication downwards to the team is that of deciding what to communicate. Information tends to come from four major sources; from headquarters, from the area manager, from other teams, from the community. There is much that can be communicated, the skill comes in choosing what it is appropriate to pass on. The cry from the ground floor may be that information is not being passed down, but if it were all to be passed on there would be no time to absorb it all and on the whole the team would not be very much the wiser.

Having selected what to communicate, the next decision which has to be made is how communication is to take place. In the first instance the team leader has the choice of passing information on verbally or in writing. If it is to go in writing it can be in the form of a memo to all staff to whom it is relevant – or it can be in the form of a notice on the noticeboard. It is probably arguable which will gain most attention.

If the information is to be passed on verbally, the team leader has first to decide which team members need the information. He must then decide whether to communicate to each individually or to the team as a whole, at a team meeting. Controversial issues need to be handled with particular care. He needs to be sure that other team leaders are passing on the same information at more or less the same time and in the same way.

The team leader may also be in difficulties when either he cannot give information because it has not yet been finally decided elsewhere but has immediate implications for practice, or when he has been directed by the hierarchy not to give the team certain information which he may feel they need because of its effect on practice.

When communicating difficult issues it is the team leader's task to represent the hierarchy's viewpoint fairly. How the team leader interprets the 'bad news' and whether he 'blames' someone elsewhere for it will be crucial to the team's acceptance. Conveying the message that as team leader, you don't agree with the decision, but it has got to be carried out is generally neither positive nor helpful. In the end it is also the team leader's task to ensure that decisions are carried out. So it pays to be positive! One of the features of middle management is that team leaders are sometimes put in the position of having to carry out decisions with which they do not agree.

(c) *Communication with peer group*

Communication on this level takes place in two ways. In the first it consists of communication between team leaders responsible for a number of teams in the same area office. The purpose of communication here is to give support to one another, to exchange information (perhaps building up an area profile), to share resources and to help out with work demands. Within such a close knit group as an area office the ability of team leaders to work with one another is of utmost importance if the rest of the staff are to work effectively together, without overlap of roles and functions and with clear ideas of area objectives. When the area office leaders meet together with the area manager the group can become a decision-making body for the area. It can be decision making without the area manager's presence, but only with the latter's permission.

The second way in which communication takes place between team leaders occurs on a wider level across the whole authority. From such communication team leaders can once more support and help one another in the carrying out of their day to day work. Ideas can be exchanged and expertise disseminated and an overall picture of the authority, its strengths and weaknesses can be obtained. One important facet of the coming together of this particular group is the pressure they can exert on higher management.

Team leaders are potentially a powerful group within the structure because of their position and number. However, if they are to be an effective pressure group they need to be well organised, positive about the issues they choose to take up and have the ability to communicate their ideas to those above.

(d) *Communication with the community*

Part of the team leader's role is a public relations task with the community itself and with other professional workers in the area. One of the difficulties of carrying out this task successfully is the current poor image and bad press from which social work is suffering. This can have the effect of making anyone who has to represent their department act, or be, on the defensive. Senior management in departments often do not define the task that they feel it is appropriate and realistic to undertake and many have unrealistic expectations of the quality and quantity of the work to be done within the limited resources available. The skill of imparting this positively is one which would tax the most able politician! Success or failure is bound up with the personal relationships the team leader builds up with individuals within the community. Once he is respected for what he is and does, the door is open for the rest of the team's work to be accepted too.

What team leaders convey in their communication will depend on where they see their loyalties, or hopefully, on whether they can maintain an appropriate balance of loyalties to their profession, their hierarchy, the professional workers in their team and to the clients they serve.

Nowhere is this dilemma more exposed than at an area staff meeting where the team leader can become the focus of conflict between his colleagues, who are expecting him to uphold their views and give them his support. The team leader who is comfortable in this situation is one who has gone most of the way to establishing himself as a middle manager, able to cope with the 'interchangeable parts' of his role. Never, in social services departments, will 'the entire problem of management' be solved, but perhaps it is possible to achieve some 'order and discipline' through team leaders who are clear about the task they are undertaking.

Author's Note:

The material for this chapter is gathered from our joint experience. Between us we have been team leaders in three authorities, and an area manager in one. More recently we have been extensively involved as lecturers on management courses with team leaders.

The Team Leader's Style of Management

Beryl Pain

The team leader and the team work are part of a large organisation which has certain structures and goals. In order to ensure that the work of the team and of individual workers fits in with those structures and enhances those goals, a pattern of management is necessary. The purpose of management is to acquire, control and direct the resources of the organisation whether those resources take the form of money, concrete services or manpower.

Before the development of the unified social services departments in 1971, the social work managers were to be found at the top of the hierarchies of the individual departments – the Childrens' Officers, the Chief Welfare Officers and their deputies. Their fundamental task was to set goals and to establish priorities for their departments and in this context they were responsible for the selection of staff, the allocation of work and the review of performance. There were also senior social workers who supervised the day by day work of other social workers – their responsibility was to ensure a high standard of performance of work by giving advice about individual cases but they did not usually take part in the management tasks referred to above. The team leaders, or 'middle managers' who emerged after the 1971 reorganisation, however, have been expected to perform both supervisory and management tasks – they not only advise and support their teams but are also accountable for their team's work to the agency. In the early 1970s when many unqualified workers were taken on by departments, the role of the middle manager became a particularly crucial one. As departments change, and some area teams now have a full complement of qualified social workers, the role of the team leader becomes more problematical – is it really necessary to have a middle manager? Moreover as social services teams become more complex, embracing a variety of staff with differing skills and abilities, not all of them social workers, what sort of role must the team leader adopt to be effective and what is the most appropriate style of management?

By "style of management" I mean not only the team leader's personal mode of behaviour – the way in which he conducts immediate social relations with colleagues and subordinates (although it includes that) – but the way in which he fulfils his role and works within the mode of functioning of the organisation[1]. Team leaders are concerned with the department's structure of control but the nature of the control may be interpreted and applied in different ways. At one extreme is the team leader who believes that he must do all the controlling and expects his workers to consult him about even minor decisions. At the other extreme is the team leader who relies on his workers exerting their own self control and imposing upon themselves whatever discipline may be required. The approach of most falls somewhere on a continuum between these two extremes. They, consciously or unconsciously, adopt the style which best fits in with their beliefs about people, their sense of accountability to the department, and their opinion about the abilities of their subordinates. The style they choose is likely to be one that minimises the impact of certain ambiguities in their role – those which arise from their middle position in the hierarchy, having to take into account both professional and organisational goals.

In this chapter I shall first explore the nature of the factors which affect the team leader's choice of style – his perception of his role, the 'culture' of his department, and the tasks performed by his subordinates. I will then go on to suggest ways in which a style can be worked out appropriate to the changing nature of the team leader's role – this will include a discussion of the implications of 'managing' professionals, the problems experienced by professionals in organisations, and the significance of emerging forms of specialisation.

1. The Team Leader's Perception of his Role

Perhaps the most important influence governing the style adopted by the team leader is the perception he has about his role arising from the nature of his professional training. Most social workers who are promoted to a job in management are given no additional training and it may be some while before they have the opportunity to reflect on how the skills needed for their new role differ from social work ones[2]. Their instinct on promotion is to react in one of two different ways. They may tend to bring to relationships with team members the casework attitudes learned during basic training – acceptance, support, reassurance. Initially it may be that the work flourishes as most workers need a certain amount of these things but there is evidence that some team members are not happy with this style and wish for more challenge and standard setting from their immediate superior[3].

Alternatively, the newly promoted manager may feel unhappy about the authority aspects of his role and uncomfortably aware of his need to know what is going on if he is to take responsibility for the work of his team. He can best deal with the anxiety thus engendered by emphasising the directive aspects of his job and he sometimes does this in a way contrary to theories about peoples' motivation learned on his professional training. He aims to reduce his own uncertainty by behaving like a traditional 'boss'.

These two instinctive reactions to the management task may be linked with an analysis made by Douglas McGregor in his book "The Human Side of Enterprise"[4]. McGregor distinguishes between two contrasting management styles which he calls Theory X and Theory Y. Theory X is the expression of traditional views of direction and control. It tends to be based on the belief that the average human being dislikes work and will avoid it if he can. Because of this, most people must be coerced, threatened with punishment, to get them to put adequate effort towards the achievement of the organisation's objectives. Furthermore, most people prefer to be directed and wish to avoid responsibility, valuing security above everything else. The adherent of Theory Y, on the other hand, considers that most people prefer to work rather than idle away their time and that if an individual is committed to the organisation's objectives he will exercise his own discretion and self-control. We tend to underestimate the individual's capabilities and potentialities.

The philosophy which lies behind Theory X is not one that is likely to be explicitly stated in an organisation where most of the workers are professionals, but nevertheless its outworkings are sometimes evident in the management/staff relationships in social services departments. The local government framework to some extent predisposes managers to adopt bureaucratic and controlling attitudes. Even amongst trained social workers the philosophy of Theory Y, while it may predominate in the attitudes which are shown to clients, is not always extended to positive attitudes towards subordinates or even colleagues. One of the purposes of management training is to enable the manager to stand back, as it were, from his work; to deliberately consider what style he is adopting; and how far this style is appropriate both to the goals of the department and to the management of the people directly responsible to him. He should then be able to make a conscious choice as to where on the continuum of control he wishes to position himself.

2. Organisational Influences

The team leader's style will be governed not only by his personal preference (whether instinctive or the result of informed choice) but by the norms and ethos of the department in which he works. While most social services departments have a hierarchical form of organisation, the importance placed on such factors as strict adherence to job descriptions, and the exact carrying out of prescribed rules and procedures may vary greatly as will relationships

41

between team leaders and their own immediate superiors. They may feel that the area manager is constantly looking over their shoulder or that they are left to get on with the job in their own way. Handy in his book "Understanding Organisations"[5] describes the different kinds of 'culture' adopted by different organisations. He distinguishes between what he calls a 'role culture' where the main emphasis is on roles to be performed and on prescribed tasks and procedures (such as is traditionally met within the Civil Service) and what he calls a 'task' culture where the organisation is flexible enough to allow groups of people with different kinds of expertise to come together to perform different specific tasks appropriate to changing circumstances. Generally speaking, the Theory X style of management is more likely to be found in a 'role' culture where there is little scope for discretion and the structure of authority is maintained by sanctions. Theory Y is more likely to be found in a 'task' culture where jobs and tasks are less predictable and where the emphasis is on the exchange of ideas between workers and managers. (As mentioned below sometimes more than one culture can exist in the organisation but in different parts).

In some social services departments deliberate attempts are made to involve fieldworkers in such matters as the development of departmental policy. By means of working parties which cut in membership terms across team and management boundaries, people at different levels in the organisation can extend their roles and contribute their expertise to considering better ways of achieving the organisation's goals. (Compare Zand.[6]) It would be too optimistic, however, to think that many departments have gone very far in this direction. Parsloe and Stevenson in their monumental work on "Social Services Teams" note from the departments they studied "the lack of imagination and creativity which would lead to attempts to redefine objectives and roles through experiment and to provide organisational structures to facilitate innovation"[7]. If the team leader is a member of his area management team he may be able to influence the running of the department along these sort of lines. In any case, he can try within his own team to put some of these principles into operation. According to how far he feels secure in his role and how far he can tolerate ambiguity and uncertainty, he will encourage the team to take part in such functions as for example the allocation of work for which he is primarily responsible. The team leader's job in interpreting the goals of the department to the team, and in representing the professional goals and opinions of team members to senior managers is often an uncomfortable one. It will be difficult for him to encourage innovation and creativity if the 'ethos' of the department militates against this. Too often he will tend either to conform to 'departmental wisdom' or to rebel against attempts to restrict his innovatory role. His responsibility for the team's work, however, particularly if it covers a particular geographical 'patch', should give him the confidence to take risks provided that these are compatible with his professional ethic and goals. Action should be accompanied both by the giving of clear information to senior management about what is taking place and by a willingness to defend his actions rationally and in terms of the goals of the department.

3. Management of workers with different tasks

The style of the team leader should be shaped not only by his personal preference and by the 'culture' of his department but by the nature of the tasks performed by his subordinates. It is now being recognised that there are two distinct kinds of tasks being carried out in social work teams[8] – these may be loosely described as 'social services' and 'social work' tasks. Burns and Stalker in their book "The Management of Innovation" suggest that one of the factors that help to decide the best kind of structure for any organisation is the nature of the tasks being carried out[9]. If these are always the same and not subject to changing circumstances, a bureaucratic type of structure and authoritarian type of control may be appropriate. This can be highly inappropriate, however, if the tasks are constantly changing to meet new circumstances and the nature of jobs cannot always be defined prior to their being carried out. Of course as Handy suggests, it is possible for two different parts of an organisation, concerned with different tasks, to adopt different 'cultures' accordingly[10].

In the Brunel University research on different 'work strata' in social services departments, a distinction has been made between workers carrying out 'prescribed tasks' and those whose skills lie in 'situational responses'[11]. The former may be described as 'social services' tasks and are concerned mainly with the provision of concrete services such as home helps, meals on wheels, aids and adaptations for handicapped people, day nursery and childminding facilities. The provision of these services takes up a large part of the social services budget – tight control must be kept on expenditure and strict criteria of client eligibility adopted. The tasks of many of the staff who man these services are prescribed ones which can be subject, to some extent, to rules and procedures. A style of management tending towards Theory X may be more applicable in these circumstances, although the competence and skills of the workers involved must also be taken into account.

'Social work' tasks, on the other hand, depend very much more on the worker responding to peoples' problems and to situations that arise in the course of casework, groupwork or community work, in a way that is appropriate at the time – not in ways that can be prescribed in advance. By means of professional relationships and by enlisting the assistance of other agencies, help is given to clients with social and psychological problems of various kinds. The task will vary according to the needs of the client, and according to the skills, interests and training of the worker. There is no one way of working that is appropriate to all situations. Social workers cannot be tightly controlled as flexibility and adaptability of response is most important. It seems that a Theory Y style of management is more appropriate in these circumstances.

A difficulty may arise if team leaders have in their teams, workers performing tasks at different levels or even the same workers performing both kinds of task. Management training should increase awareness of these kinds of factors to be considered in relation to management style and so help team leaders in developing the skills necessary to respond in differential ways. The team leader will need to balance the individual workers' capabilities with the demands of the job he is called on to do, and the degree of supervision necessary will vary accordingly.

4. The Management of Professionals

Team Leaders need to develop a style that is consistent with the management of professional workers who possess various kinds of skill and expertise and the following factors must be considered in this connection.

A. *Supervision and the 'autonomous' worker*

It is now generally recognised that the more experienced the worker, the more leeway he should be given for making his own decisions about his work. Hey and Rowbottom discuss the concepts of 'delegated discretion' versus 'professional autonomy'[12]. They suggest that for each worker there will be "some optimum degree of direction and support suited to his particular needs". The recent BASW paper on "Alternative Structures"[13] goes so far as to suggest that the time will come when a qualified and experienced social worker who asks for a resource for a client, which he believes is necessary on casework grounds, should not be turned down just because his manager disagrees with his professional judgement, but only for some other reason such as, presumably, lack of the resource.

B. *The trend towards specialisation*

In the present situation it is usual and desirable for the experienced worker to

44

consult his team leader before making important decisions, but the trend towards specialisation either according to work method or according to client group, will make the situation more complex. A worker may develop expertise in a particular area of work that goes beyond the knowledge and resources of his immediate superior. He may need to relate to some specialist in another team or to higher management for consultation. The team leader may find it difficult to see how he can be accountable for the work of such specialists but if the boundaries of the work of the team are defined for example according to a 'patch' system[14] then flexible ways must be found of allowing such cross-team consultation to happen. It is possible to envisage a situation where the team leader manages a team comprising (among other members) an intermediate treatment specialist who relates for consultation to a departmental I.T. organiser; a health care worker attached to a GP practice who relates to a health care specialist in higher management; a fostering and adoption specialist who relates to a professional adviser etc. (Compare here the work on 'co-ordinative' relationships and on 'dual influence' situations[15]). The team leader will need to develop a style that is consistent with the distribution of power. The worker may have the power of specialist knowledge; the team leader has the power and responsibility to manage the work of the area and to see that client need is adequately met.

C. *Accountability and Responsibility*

Parsloe and Stevenson note the amount of confusion in the minds of both social workers and team leaders about this issue[16] and their study shows most team leaders recognised their own accountability to the department for the work of their team but seemed remarkably relaxed about this, to the extent that they did not seem to recognise the full implications and take enough steps to inform themselves of what was going on. Most social workers, on the other hand, felt that the responsibility for their cases was theirs – although recognising the agency's overall accountability for their work as expressed through the management structure. What many most feared could happen was another "Maria Colwell" case[17] where they, as individual workers, might be called upon to account in public for something from which even the most supportive department might not be able to protect them. The authors comment "few social workers or senior staff had been able to develop structures and managerial techniques which offered in the words of one social worker, 'protection with autonomy'".

If protection and autonomy are in any sense to be combined, it is essential that better systems of assessment of work, accreditation of workers, and staff development programmes are set up in social services departments. Open and honest communication can then take place in an atmosphere of co-operation and trust which can promote the dual goal.

D. *Professionals and the Organisation*

The problem for managers in social services departments (as for the management of professionals in any organisation) is to know how best to harness the energies of the professional worker in order to ensure that their skills are put to the best use in the service of the agency. Social workers' primary loyalty is usually to their clients and some seem to find it hard to accept the compromises that working in a publicly accountable organisation entails. Some tend to over-perform in pursuit of personal and professional aims. The high standards they set themselves may result in their spending much time with categories of clients who are not a priority from the department's point of view. Some boundaries need to be set around the professionals and the way they use their time. They are themselves one of the agency's resources and it is the job of the manager to see that manpower resources, as much as any other kind of resources, are used in the best possible way. Moreover, there are some areas of work (notably in areas connected with the deprivation of liberty, such as mental health, or matters of life and death, such as non-accidental injury where even 'autonomous' workers must follow certain rules and procedures because of the agency's overall accountability to the general public.

The problems surrounding the management of professionals is one being faced by a number of organisations and it is thrown into sharp relief for instance in the Army which has had an influx of people such as engineers, technical experts, accountants and other specialists, and where there has traditionally been a regime of authoritarian, bureaucratic control. It is recognised that such professionals cannot be controlled according to the style of Theory X but the problem of ensuring that their goals are harmonised with those of the organisation is not easy and ways of doing this have yet to be worked out. The problem also arises in institutes of research where heads of groups need to exercise the right kind of coordination and goal setting in order to avoid a situation of chaos engendered by everyone going ahead and doing 'their own thing'. A Theory Y style of management is obviously applicable to the management of professionals but how is it to be worked out in practice?

There is a system which has been used in some parts of industry, mainly for use among managers, which seems worth discussing for the clues it may provide to some of the problems of 'autonomy', supervision, accountability and over-performance affecting professionals as outlined above. The system known as 'management by objectives' has been thought by some experts not to be applicable to the public services for reasons which will be outlined, but its basic principles seem well worth considering bearing in mind that it may be misused if one section in an organisation attempts to use it to gain their own ends.

5. Management by Objectives (M.B.O.)

This approach was initially developed by Drucker[18] and later by Humble in his book of that title[19]. According to Humble 'what is needed is a principle of management that will give full scope to *individual strength* and responsibility and at the same time give *common direction* of vision and effort, establish teamwork and harmonise the goals of the individual with the common weal''. M.B.O. is a system that tries to integrate the organisation's goals of efficient service with the professional's need to contribute and develop himself personally. A worker and his superior (perhaps social worker and team leader) sit down together and debate constructively objectives, standards, controls and improvement ideas and meet regularly to appraise progress and problems. To relate this idea to a social work team, this may be an exercise to be conducted in a group discussion of the needs of an area; the best way to deploy members of the team to cope with referrals; the building up of common standards of assessment, investigation, recordkeeping and response to client need; the development of new ways of working. Discussion of the progress of ongoing cases, groups and work in the community will contribute to the management task of review of work accomplished. The team can then be seen not just as a collection of individuals who are individually accountable to the team leader but as a group of equal workers who together with their manager are jointly accountable to the agency for their response to client need in a particular area.

The attempt to apply this system in the public services has been open to a numbers of criticisms[20], [21]. The impression has been created that far from fitting in with a Theory Y style of management, the system is likely to be used by senior managers to impose bureaucratic controls. This they may do rather than allow 'grass roots' workers, by means of the system, to influence the running of the organisation and to take part in constructive discussion about aims and objectives. It is also argued that managers may use M.B.O. to achieve consensus and phase out discussion of conflicting aims and values, and that M.B.O. tends to result in the narrowing down of objectives rather than in the opening up of new horizons. It is of course possible for this to happen if it is operated by managers uncommitted to a Theory Y style. Another reason however, why it could result in this is because of the difficulties encountered within social work in setting professional standards which are in any sense measurable in terms of goals achieved. Thus James[22] outlines objectives which appear to be essentially administrative ones – concerned with concrete ways of dealing with cases such as frequency of client contact and numbers of supervision sessions necessary in order to ensure adequate standards of work. This is a criticism which can also be levied against the system of caseload management now in operation in some social services department[23]. The emphasis in the setting of priorities tends to centre round administrative criteria such as the amount of time that needs to be spent on each case each week (surely a changing variable if ever there was one).

Social workers have always been reluctant to measure the effect of their work with clients in accurate ways involving acute observations of changes in attitudes and behaviour, and this has led to the kind of criticisms of 'woolly thinking' and 'unsubstantiated claims' made against the profession by Brewer and Lait in their recent book[24]. (This was to some extent countered by Colin Pritchard in an article in "Community Care"[25].)

If any system of objective setting is to be effective in the context of the social work team, it must involve the setting of professional as well as organisational goals and it must provide an opportunity for the conflict between the two to be discussed. Rightly used it can become a means for the bringing together of personal and organisational aims and this will happen as much by workers pressing their views on management as vice-versa. As resources become more scarce, it is likely that more and more pressure will come from politicians and others for evidence justifying the employment of expensive trained workers and the reasons given for doing so must be backed up by constructive appraisal of work being accomplished. Social workers must develop effective criteria for measuring change in individuals, group and communities. If they themselves do not have the ability to do research they should be able to seek help from those who have the training and time to do it. The team, as a group of workers with similar interests but different kinds of skill and expertise can become a forum for such appraisal.

6. Skills and Training for the Team Leader

If the team is to work effectively in this sort of way, the team leader will need to develop skills in team-building such as are described in other chapters of this

48

book. Whether or not some system such as M.B.O. is adopted as an appropriate way of fulfilling professional goals, the team leader must develop a style that is consistent with the management of professionals and specialists. The 'functional' approach to leadership, described by Adair[26], stresses that leadership is essentially interaction between the leader, group members and the situation (which in our context must include the organisation). The emphasis in this approach is not so much on what the leader is, or what he does, but on his ability to provide the necessary functions in a manner acceptable to the group. He describes these functions as those of planning, supporting, initiating, controlling, informing and evaluating. In order to develop these abilities all managers need to undergo further training after completion of CQSW or CSS studies. This training should include the development of skills necessary for leadership, especially an understanding of the causes of conflict in groups and organisations and a knowledge of the strategies and tactics necessary to cope with it[27].

7. The Demise of the Team Leader?

The BASW Working Party interim report on "Alternative Structures"[28] envisages that the day may not be long in coming when the team leader is no longer needed. This view seems to be based on the belief not that management as a form of control is no longer needed but that it can be shared by a group of professionals as a kind of extra task on top of their social work tasks. There seems to be no allowance made for the fact that the two roles are very different ones and that the skills are not always found in the same person. Unfortunately social services departments have always suffered from this misapprehension – hence the appointment to so many senior positions of people who were once excellent social workers but who are now ineffective managers. There should of course, be a career structure in fieldwork for such workers without their having to go into management.

The particular way in which the team leader is needed will depend to some extent on whether area social work teams support systems of 'patch' working. If this trend continues, with the opportunities it brings for the utilisation of resources within the community, the team leader of the future is likely to co-ordinate a group of specialists working in a particular geographical area and using a variety of social work methods. Within the team, goals will be set and priorities decided which will contribute to the formation of area and departmental policy. The team leader's role will become more developmental and innovatory and his job will become more important not because he has more say in what his workers do or decide but because the management of a

49

group of professionals and others with varying skills, abilities and knowledge, is a skilled job demanding a willingness to take risks and to experiment with new methods of work. If team leaders do *not* respond to the style of management needed, it may be that the forecast of their imminent demise will come true.

Acknowledgement

I wish to acknowledge the help given me in connection with this chapter particularly in relation to section 4 (D) by Cliff Fishenden, sometime Senior Lecturer in the Department of Behavioural Studies, Newcastle-upon-Tyne Polytechnic.

References

1. Fox, Alan, *Organisational Design and Management Style.* Personnel Review Vol. No. 1 Autumn 1971.
2. Parsloe P. and Stevenson O., *Social Services Teams,* H.M.S.O. 1978, chap. 8: 64. p. 214.
3. Parsloe, P. and Stevenson, O., ibid. chap. 8: 86 pp. 220-221.
4. McGregor, Douglas. *The Human Side of Enterprise,* McGraw Hill, 1960.
5. Handy, Charles B. *Understanding Organisations,* Penguin 1976, chap. 7.
6. Zand, Dale E. *Collateral Organisation; a New Change Strategy,* Journal of Applied Behavioural Science, Vol. 10, No. 1, 1974.
7. Parsloe and Stevenson, ibid. Chap. 13: 102. p. 328.
8. Report of B.A.S.W. Working Party. *The Social Work Task,* 1977.
9. Burns, T. and Stalker, J. M. *The Management of Innovation,* Tavistock 1966.
10. Handy, ibid. p. 199.
11. Rowbottom, R. W. and Billis D. *The Stratification of Work and Organisational Design,* "Organising Social Services Departments" (chap. 1) Heinemann 1980.
12. *Social Services Departments,* B.I.O.S.S. Heinemann 1974 pp. 100-110.
13. B.A.S.W. Working Party. *Alternative Structures,* Interim Report October 1979 (unpub).
14. Hadley, R. and McGrath, M. Bedford Square Press, 1980.
15. Working Paper, *Social Work Practices, Careers and Organisation in Area Teams,* B.I.O.S.S. 1978.
16. Parsloe and Stevenson, ibid., chap. 8: 101 p. 224.
17. Report of the Committee of Inquiry into the Care and Supervision provided in relation to Maria Colwell, D.H.S.S. 1974.
18. Drucker, Peter F. *The Practice of Management,* Heinemann 1955.
19. Humble, John. *Management by Objectives,* Gower Press 1972.
20. James, R. L. *Management by Objectives, Social Work Today.* Vol. 6, No. 21, 22.1.76.
21. Miller, C. and Scott, T. Letter to *Social Work Today.* Vol. 6, No. 24, 4.3.76.
22. James, R. L., ibid.
23. Vickery, A. *Caseload Management: A Guide for Supervision of Social Work Staff,* N.I.S.W. Papers 1977.
24. Brewer, C. and Lait, J. *Can Social Work Survive?* Temple Smith 1980.
25. Pritchard, C. "What is Social Work Trying to Do?" *Community Care* 11.12.80.
26. Adair, J. *Training for Leadership,* Gower Press 1978.
27. Handy, ibid. chap. 8.
28. B.A.S.W. Working Party. *Alternative Structures,* ibid.

Social Workers' Expectations of their Team Leader
Bill Bennett

"What's a boss anyway, just a misunderstanding"
from 'Les Bas Fonds', Renoir.

Introduction

When I first applied for a post as team leader in a social services area office, I was asked to attend an informal interview with the team. Though this took place cordially and over lunch in a pub, I was left in no doubt as to the critical nature of the gathering. Out of the wide-ranging discussion which took place, one question seemed to lie at the heart of the matter. "What would you do if there was an urgent case to allocate, say a court report, and we all had such heavy caseloads and commitments that each of us, with justification, refused to take it on?" It took some time to respond as I remember being flooded with ambivalent and emotionally charged feelings generated by my fantasies and fears of their expectations. Combined with the challenge to my possible future authority I also detected in the question more than a touch of anger about their felt low status and frustrations. Would I support the team and in turn challenge line management about the unreasonable pressure of work experience at field level; or would I 'pass the buck'. Whatever other function they might have expected from the team leader, it was my first realization of distance being placed between myself and the members of this team and of their demand for a manager.

As an example of one crucial area of team relations, this episode serves to highlight some of the dilemmas that exist in area offices over the division of responsibilities, and in particular over the allocation of work. In addition, it demonstrates some of the prevailing attitudes and perceptions that remain within field social work today.

The issue of responsibility lies at the core of this paper. Therefore I will begin with a brief discussion of this concept and how it relates to social work practice in area based teams. This will be demonstrated in practical terms by a description of two of the major influences which affect team relationships namely departmental expectations and resource allocation. The next section will contain a broad appraisal of the expectations that social workers have of their team leaders; pinpointing some of the more crucial implications for daily practice and for role relationships within a team. By examining the dysfunctional aspects of this generally accepted pattern of expectations, I will identify those areas which I believe are not conducive to good field work practice. Drawing on my own work experience, I will then delineate the social work beliefs and the understanding of responsibility in social work that to my mind form the ingredients of teamwork. It is my experience that the adoption of these beliefs and attitudes considerably alter the expectations that social workers have of their team leaders; in effect creating a very different model of teamwork from the one that is often to be found in social services departments. I will discuss the implications of adopting this different model (which I shall call a 'team approach'), and finally examine some of the constraints that may be encountered. Throughout I will be restricting my comments to those which apply to social services area based offices. However, I believe the issues to be discussed are of wider application, and are not without relevance to those working outside this setting.

Social services area teams contain many regional and local differences. For my purposes, I am going to consider a typical team of workers, based in an area or district office alongside two or three similar teams and all under the auspices of a principal officer. Such a team may comprise a team leader, five social workers, perhaps a trainee, a social work assistant, and an occasional student. An occupational therapist, home help organiser or community worker may also be attached. I will not be concerned with particular types of teams, for example, intake or long-term, though later comments will support a model of teams working to small and defined catchment areas. Whilst all teams enjoy some degree of colleague suppport, I will assume that the focus of work is case-oriented; with team members in the main working individually. (An assumption supported by the findings of Stevenson and Parsloe, who came to the conclusion, "So far as daily work was concerned, then the fact is that the majority of team members went about their 'case work' as individuals, formally relating to their senior, 'the captain'[1]."

Responsibility

Within social services departments an issue often raised is whether social workers are primarily responsible to the local authority or to their clients. However this argument has little to recommend it; not only does it misunderstand the day to day realities of field social work but the confusion that follows is often compounded by the use of the term 'accountable' as if it were interchangeable with 'responsible'. It is not surprising that discussions around this issue are seldom fruitful. Here an analysis of what is meant by 'responsibility' can inject some clarity into our definition of accountability. Leiserson[2] says of responsibility that it, ". . . implies answerability for performance of an office, charge or duty," and he divided the focus of use into four areas:–

(a) accountability – this is solely related to 'duties', for example to those contained in job descriptions and agreed in contracts of employment.

(b) discretionary capacity – this means for that which is delegated, or authority expected over and above the responsibilities for 'duties',

(c) to professional group – this includes beliefs, ethics, integrity, allegiances to particular bodies of knowledge, a commitment to training and a responsibility for standards of practice,

(d) in terms of loyalty – this can be to colleagues, the department, to clients, to the neighbourhood, or to oneself.

Here it can be noted that the issue of accountability is also fundamentally based with the public; for it is their elected representatives who have decided to appoint the managers to whom we are accountable, and with good reason. The procedural aspects of the department are basically designed to avoid malpractice or favouritism.

These four areas, whilst not mutually exclusive, provide an essential framework for a discussion of social work responsibilities; a discussion which once digested can lead to a better understanding of the context within which social workers practise. So how do social workers view their responsibilities? Stevenson and Parsloe concluded that ". . . a large number of social workers in all areas were primarily concerned with their freedom to relate to clients in the way they thought most appropriate. They were ready to see the acquisition of resources for their clients as an individualistic confrontation between themselves and the resource controllers 'out there', and felt that it was inappropriate to devote much of their time to efforts to influence wider resource allocation decisions"[3]. This prevailing attitude stems from two major factors. Firstly, until recent years, social work training has been predominantly concerned with client/worker relationships, with little emphasis on how social workers can develop an influential role within their organizations. Secondly, this development has been compounded by the feelings of impotence at basic grade level which come from working in large bureaucratic organizations.

It has become increasingly more difficult to work against this trend, as certain patterns of departmental communications have grown up which serve to maintain this situation. Firstly, there are the expectations made of team leaders by departmental line management. On a practical level these include taking delegated authorization for financial and service provision, accountability for keeping to policy lines, knowledge of cases held and an intimate understanding of work flow within the team. Central to these expectations is a responsibility for monitoring referrals, allocating work and disseminating information. Much of this work is very necessary to the management role; however, in my opinion, it leads to too great an emphasis being placed on the team leader to act as spokesman both for the team, and individually for its members. Often the language used in area offices supports this emphasis. For example, when I first became team leader, the team was known as 'Bill's group'. In turn management decisions to restrict circulation of certain 'confidential' departmental information can only serve to reinforce the role definition. This practice usually results in social workers feeling undervalved, let down by their team leader and embarrassed in their contacts with other council departments, outside agencies and the public.

Secondly, there is the system of local authority resource allocation. Continuation of existing service provision and agreement to further capital expenditure are subject to budgetry control, and allocation of funds by different departmental committees of councillors, usually takes place on a competitive basis. As far as social services is concerned, proposals are generally made on the basis of a shortage of departmental provision, (this could be embodied in waiting lists for domiciliary services such as meals on wheels or home helps, or in vacancy rates at residential or day care establishments), with little emphasis on alternative methods of work or on the promotion of community resources. This attitude permeates through to team level where in the face of the high 'bombardment of requests', such is the need to be seen to be covering statutory duties, that the concentration of hierarchical attention and support often goes to bolster up those teams who are struggling to survive, irrespective of whether their difficulties are principally due to bad management or real pressures. This means that those teams which in the face of day to day pressures develop good morale and efficient ways of working often end up penalised. Benefits can be gained from claiming to be in a 'poor state', not only to attract resources but as an excuse for many ills. The overriding effect on the quality of service, however, is one of diminishing returns for extra effort.

Between teams the attitudes which derive from the factors I have described, can lead to rivalry and envy. Workers frustrated by the 'low mileage' in trying

54

to improve matters begin to adopt an 'over the fence' attitude, looking to see if other teams are getting an unfair share of resources. Within teams, field-workers experience many feelings of ambivalence, wanting on the one hand to develop skills and promote a caring service whilst at the same time finding that it is this element of altruism which leaves them open to a 'trade in guilt'. (A form of inter-agency blackmail which attempts to persuade social workers to undertake a course of action on behalf of their clients which is not usually part of the treatment plans but solely designed to prevent their clients from being penalised in such a way that might only serve to increase the risk of family disintegration e.g. fuel disconnection, court action, suspension from school, withdrawal of day nursery place and so on). Using the social worker as a receptacle for inadequacies is also the means by which other agencies can avoid having to negotiate directly with clients.

As a result of these factors many workers fall back to stating that one of their main tasks is in direct work to "prevent clients from suffering". These feelings fundamentally affect the relationship between social workers and their team leaders, where the latter present as accessible targets both for feelings of ambivalence and for many fieldworkers' hopes, aspirations and expectations.

The Generally Accepted Model in Social Services Departments

In the main, social workers' expectations are contained within four major functions of the team leader role, namely:–

(a) to obtain resources for the team,

(b) to obtain resources for 'clients' and to ration their provision in terms of availability and agreed criteria,

(c) to promote professional development of team members,

(d) to administer the requests, referrals and information received by the team and be available for advice, supervision and consultation.

They are each worthy of closer examination.

(a) Many social workers expend considerable time and effort in demanding additional resources for their team. The rationale behind this is that good conditions of service are essential if clients are to be offered a reasonable standard of practice. They also indicate the level to which the local authority values social work. Here social workers will expect their representative, the team leader, to become a skilled negotiator at area management meetings, and to plead that their team is a special case in its need for resources which can range from increases in staffing and administrative support to the provision of desks, stapling machines or photocopying facilities. Decisions about the allocation of resources can be difficult. For example, if an area officer is allocated a community work post, should this be placed say in a team which has been preparing for this eventuality, or in a team which is short of staff, suffering from low morale and in need of a boost.

It should be noted that many social work teams look no further than getting their 'fair share'. They may not be particularly adept at determining priorities about what resources they need or in how to go about obtaining them. Although it is right for the team to expect their 'leader' to play a major part in this task, unless the team as a whole accepts the need for some new resource and prepares for its integration into the team then at worst it will feel like an imposition whilst at best its use may not be maximised to the full.

(b) Team leaders spend much of their time acting as 'gate keepers' to the allocation of resources, and their signature is often the 'passport' to the provision of funds or services for clients. In addition not all resources are allocated at the discretion of the team leader and in these circumstances social workers may expect the support and direct intervention of the team leader in canvassing the relevant principal officer or in attending case conferences where allocation decisions are made. In both events social workers can expect of their team leader some understanding of client/worker relationships and knowledge of relevant departmental policy and criteria for provision of services. This may sound relatively straightforward; yet it is an area which can create considerable conflict, a conflict fundamentally based on the combination of the authoratitive and supportive roles expected of the team leader. Here, a number of factors come into play:–

(1) Hidden messages may be contained within social workers' applications for resources. They may be finding it hard to say 'no' to their clients and really looking to their team leader to take this decision for them.

(2) Many workers, including team leaders, believe that the strict criteria on which is based the allocation of council services do not accurately represent what is generally publicized as available. For example it is left to the social workers to dash the hopes of elderly people who had

been led to believe often by elected members that a telephone was theirs for the asking.

(3) Many of the resources required are not available. Often the team leader is expected to absorb frustrations, take the knocks for service limitations and on occasions to conjure up the next possible solution. Because the team leader is also likely to have an intimate knowledge of the needs and stresses which obtain in particular cases, this reality testing can be one of the most difficult expectations to meet.

(c) In Stevenson and Parsloe's studies many of the social workers interviewed saw the team leader as the person responsible for the promotion of their professional development[4]. Social workers therefore expect their team leader to be aware of their individual requirements for skill development. This will mean keeping workers' personal interests in mind as well as looking out for training opportunities and relevant practical experiences. This process often begins with the expectations of team leaders to induct new members and play a major role in helping them integrate into the team. (Malcolm Payne's contribution to this book deals substantially with staff development and the team leader's contribution).

Central to this area is the formal, one to one supervision of social workers by their team leader. At these sessions, and in addition to discussions about their professional development, social workers will expect to receive consultation about cases and methods of work. For many social workers this is a crucial area; it is the place where treatment plans are made or where in difficult circumstances they are assured they have done all they can. It is also the place where they are asked to account for their work and where 'over-involvement' with clients can be brought to check. There are therefore high expectations of the team leader to be skilled in offering supervision, and many social workers complaints about their 'seniors' are often due to frustration with this very personal and critical relationship. The expectations of social workers about team leaders in supervision is the subject of a paper by Stephen Nixon in this book. He has some findings which suggest that social workers are critical of the level and breadth of practice wisdom of team leaders.

(d) In terms of the management of referrals and requests received at the area office social workers will expect their team leader to develop an overview of work flow so as to provide the context within which initial allocation and operational decisions can be made. In addition a protective role will be expected, ensuring that at area management meetings the team receives only its fair share of area workload. Overall, the team leader will be required to recognise team potential and plan for changes in staffing or resources.

In many teams, allocation of cases will take place at team 'allocation meetings'. In some teams, decision-making is facilitated by a team knowledge of each member's pressures and capabilities, a process crucial to team meetings. However, where this understanding has not been well developed, this meeting can become quite difficult; and the social worker who best resists taking on additional work is the one who can cope with group silence and pressures, exercising great skill in avoiding eye contact. Although for most teams, the ultimate responsibility remains firmly vested in the team leader, 'good' allocation meetings can fulfill an additional positive training function. A further expectation is that the team leader will be available, particularly at times of crises, to offer advice, have knowledge of appropriate resources, and at times act jointly with the social worker in dealing with particularly difficult cases.

In addition to the expectations described in each of these four areas, there are those of a more general nature. Firstly, the degree to which a team leader will be expected to exercise authority and discretion will very much depend on the level of experience, qualifications, skills and knowledge contained within the team. Secondly, it is important to note the part played by 'personality'. Team leaders will be expected to combine successfully all Webb's styles of leadership, namely 'bureaucratic', 'collegial' and 'charismatic'[5]; in fact as one Senior Child Care Officer once remarked to me, to be "all things to all people". In particular, social workers have an expectation to be stimulated, to be led and to be inspired.

Finally, team leaders are expected by line management *and* social workers alike to take their place in a position of lower middle management, to ration resources, to keep administrative and professional issues in harmony, to accept accountability for the handling of the cases, to relate information about policy and resources up and down the line and to hold some energy in reserve for the next crisis. Indeed to practice all the prestige and power of a 'foreman' taking a large share of the discretional responsibility for the day to day workings of the team.

The Deficiencies of this Model

In terms of departmental accountability, this model of team relations places the team leader in a pivotal position which, as far as the team is concerned, ensures that the role has many directive elements. It supports an individual and office-based approach to work with clients which does not easily lend itself to the development of teamwork as outlined later in this paper.

These factors can have serious implications for fieldwork practice:–

(a) there is often little movement by the team as a whole toward defining its own policy to resource allocation. In addition to the internal conflict, this can result in poor consistancy of response to neighbourhood expectations leading to loss of public confidence in social work,

(b) there is little effort put into determining *team* priorities. This renders the team extremely susceptible to the whims and vagaries of departmental expectations,

(c) if a team member becomes involved in a particular interest, or if the team is allocated additional resource, for example a community worker, there is little commitment or responsibility *as a whole* to the transaction; indeed the expectation is that the team leader will take the major supportive role, which, may again contribute to an individualised mode of practice.

(d) as Stevenson and Parsloe say, "... few teams we visited seemed aware of their potential as a pressure group for bringing about change within their own organisation . . ."[6].

When taken together these implications act as obstacles to the team leader's attempts to keep the 'tide at bay'. In addition they serve to generate the belief amongst social workers that they are under-valued, rarely consulted, and that their own attempts at innovation are very much limited by the capacity of their particular team leader both to understand the methodology required and to create the room and permission within line management. Further, those implications can render social workers ineffective in matters which are of vital concern to the needs of a neighbourhood, whether this be resource allocation to people in need or the promotion of participation by community groups. Above all they withhold from social workers the right to manage their own responsibilities. In these circumstances there is a vital need for a model of practice which integrates the realities of working with a neighbourhood with the workings of a team.

Teamwork Model

The following description of a 'team approach' to a neighbourhood is based on my own experiences of seven years as a team leader in a community based sub-office. This model represents one attempt to alleviate some of the deficiencies previously outlined whilst retaining as many as possible of the beneficial and necessary aspects of conventional practice; though the latter are now placed in a more corporate setting. By way of introduction, I would like to return briefly to the concept of responsibility as defined in the earlier section of this paper, namely in terms of 'accountability', 'discretional capacity', 'professional group' and 'loyalty'.

All members of an area team have the management task of integrating into their daily work the parts of their overall responsibility which appropriately belong to each of these areas. However, the extent to which this is acknowledged is open to question. The part which prompts most fieldwork discussion is the area of discretion.

In this regard the Brunel studies (1974) found, "Virtually without exception all staff in the social services with whom we have seriously discussed this issue . . . have unhesitatingly concluded after due consideration that the interaction of social workers in social services departments is one of exercising delegated discretion rather than professional autonomy"[7]. Whilst it can be said that in recent years, reduction in staff mobility, additional basic and post-qualifying training opportunities, the development of specialisation and acquisition of more practice experience have all contributed to greater professional awareness, the political and administrative needs of the organisation still bear heavily on the shoulders of fieldworkers. It remains not uncommon for fieldworkers to believe that whilst they might pay careful dues to their accountability, any respect by 'management' for their expertise and knowledge is tarnished by a prevailing attitude rooted in a 'pecking-order'. If fieldworkers are to endeavour to make practice as relevant to local need as it is to departmental procedures then that practice must be rooted in the neighbourhood. This will have the effect of increasing *that* authority within the team which comes from gaining a first hand comprehensive knowledge of the concerns and needs of the neighbourhood, enabling appropriate dues to be paid to 'accountability', 'delegated discretion' and 'professional autonomy'. In practice this means that workers are directed to acknowledge responsibility both for the foreseeable results of their *actions,* and for those areas of work they decide not to undertake. This will not be without conflict; but rather than based in the confused and ambiguous notions of accountability depicted earlier, it will increasingly be rooted in a realistic synthesis of team responsibilities.

How can synthesis be achieved? One essential task is for the team to establish a system for 'collective priority testing'[8]. Recalling my own experience, we began by asking questions:–

(1) How essential is the task or referral?

(2) Is it an appropriate one for us?

(3) Have all the relevant people been consulted and is outside help available?

(4) If we were to establish a contract, have we the time, the resources, skills and knowledge to make a worthwhile contribution – in other words, can we keep our side of the bargain?

(5) Do we need to seek further information or training and if so who will do it, how and where?

(6) How agreed are we as a team, or to reach a decision, do we first need to evaluate team perspectives and team consciousness.

This process we increasingly based within a team philosophy[9], namely:–

(1) A team has responsibility to offer services to a neighbourhood and to be a resource for that neighbourhood.

(2) There are many untapped resources in a neighbourhood.

(3) Development of skills and methods of work should be directly related to the needs that are presented.

(4) People have a right to workers who know what they are doing, and why.

(5) People have skills and given the opportunity can establish and administer resources for themselves.

(6) Status should be given to all areas and methods of work that make a contribution both directly and indirectly to the work in a neighbourhood.

As a result there was a change in the way responsibilities had previously been shared amongst team members. Individually we progressively took responsibility for the management aspects of our workload, for our position in the organisation and for our own professional development (recognising the need to seek out knowledge and skills), whilst collectively responsibility was taken for the work flow through the office. Although this style of working was to some extent out of line with normal departmental practice, management was kept informed of innovative developments, whilst internally the team ensured that it met its statutory responsibilities. By developing trust in this way we acquired an increase in autonomy which allowed the room for the team to determine priorities and its methods of work. There are considerable implications here for the team leader, and these, including changes in relationship with line management are discussed in the next section.

In retrospect, it is not possible to move towards the adoption of this framework without at the same time learning to work as a team and the above discussion lends some advice to that process. However a full discussion of this topic is outside my brief, but in this context it is useful to make some general comments. Firstly, to be effective, the shifts in responsibility I have outlined need to be *deliberately* employed and subject to continual evaluation. Secondly, day to day office administration should be geared to support professional decision-making. Finally, the team has to establish a system for setting its own priorities within the context of departmental constraints and resources.

In practice, and in addition to the usual functions of an area team, the 'team approach' means becoming involved in many different areas of work. These could include community group work, developing working relationships with local agencies, for example a general practice, influencing departmental policy, attending inter-departmental meetings and in contributing to local community development such as planning use of open space. In our experience, this entailed adopting a wider range of roles than had previously been the case. For example, acting as 'spokesman' for social services to tenants, agencies and other council departments, acting as 'executive' in team decision-making and developing both formal and informal 'consultancy' skills. The approach does not suit all workers who may feel the loss of some individuality. It can also be a difficult team to join, though new members usually find the effort worthwhile. The benefits for the team have been in high morale and low turnover of staff, and there has been an increased ability to tolerate confronting relationships with colleagues and an exposure of work. Finally, there has been our belief in the development of a balanced, consistent and yet flexible approach to the neighbourhood. This ability requires good team communications, again too wide a topic for this article, but a process which can be facilitated by viewing the team in terms of four models.

Firstly, the team can act as a 'family', sharing meals, enjoying banter and going on outings. It can allow the expression of pleasure and anger, but remain solid under external pressure. Secondly, a team can be viewed as a co-ordinated workforce, combining efficiency with flexibility of approach and multiplity of method. Thirdly, it can act as a unit within the organisation; a power-base both to bring about change and to express well documented and worked-out opinions. Lastly, as a unit within the neighbourhood, this entails the exercise of a high degree of integrity, the promotion of community participation and a high level of accessibility to agencies and the public. In the same way that individual team members need to manage the different areas of responsibility that are central to their task, here the level of sophistication in 'teamwork' reached by a team can be seen by how successfully it can almost imperceptably change models as appropriate. These two management tasks are to my mind fundamental to a 'team approach' to a neighbourhood.

The adoption of a 'team approach' has critical implications for the role of team leader and for social work expectations. The following two questions are central to this discussion:–

(1) How much should a team's character be determined by the personality and leadership style of the team leader, and how much can a team determine its own character?

(2) How subservient should the team leader be to team decisions, particularly in terms of being delegated tasks, and what rights of veto have to remain?

The Effect of Adopting a 'Team Approach' on the Workers Expections of their Team Leader

From the outset, the first expectation of the team leader will be to implement some of the administrative changes required.

This is a fair and realistic expectation, for until the team and its individual members have perceived the role changes implicit in this approach and developed the confidence necessary for their adoption, the team leader will probably be the only team member with sufficient hierarchical standing to see the changes through. Here, strength of conviction and belief in the value and status of field social work is a very desirable quality in a team leader, for there will be a need to hold firm to principles whilst *all* team members go through a period of learning and growth. As the team 'gels' it will also be expected of the team leader to promote and allow development both in social workers, and in new methods of work. This means that all areas of work have to be valued, not just the caseload, and that workers will talk primarily of their workload rather than their caseload.

This shift comes about primarily from the team becoming increasingly aware of a wider role in the neighbourhood; a role which comes from putting the team philosophy into practice. A further crucial factor is for the team to value all its members' contributions, and to recognise that the team is its members. Here the team leader has a crucial role both in encouraging and monitoring innovative schemes and in performing well in the 'buffer zone' between fieldwork practice and management. For the team leader the art is in picking up cues which assist the task of holding back some areas of work to allow others to flourish. Overall it is essential that this process is recognised and sanctioned by team meetings. Taking on new areas of work brings with it changes in role relationships within the team. Here the expectations of the team leader will be to monitor and co-ordinate these changes until they become incorporated into the team's way of working. It should be noted that these social work expectations of the team leader will diminish as the team develops its own abilities in these areas.

As has been indicated, one major result of these changes is that the team will be drawn toward promoting community resources and entering into joint working relationships with local agencies. To facilitate this work an expectation of social workers in the team will be for the team leader to become involved in local community development. This will involve learning how to obtain funds, for example 'seeding money' for self-help groups; and as local issues arise, the team leader will be increasingly drawn into working on an inter-departmental level.

The third major change in expectations occurs in the zone which lies between management and team, the 'buffer zone'. I have previously outlined this lower middle management position in terms of dissemination of information and resource allocation. For the team leader the emphasis on this area of work now diminishes as the whole team takes up a collective concern in these issues. However, social workers will still expect the team leader to take up a key position in this 'buffer zone' but with an additional change in purpose. The task will now include accounting departmentally for *team* priorities, policies, beliefs and modes of practice. This is in order to create room for the team to widen its approach, try out new ideas and develop some influence at community and organizational levels.

Finally, changes in expectation will be caused by the shift toward team self-determination; a creative process dependent on an acceptance of all members' contributions made with good intent and based on their knowledge and experience. This allows for the growth of a team philosophy and team character that is not dependent on any one member. Here it is important for example that team meetings are the 'team's' and not the 'senior's', and whilst decisions have to be made within the context of departmental constraints and job descriptions, their implications for practice should be binding on all members, including the team leader. Self-determination also means that in terms of sharing out the office workload, all members receive an appropriate level of delegation from the team which is in line with team priorities. For the team leader this is only possible if what is entailed in the role is discussed with all team members.

How does this work in practice? As an example, a team leader may be nominated by the area officer to sit on a departmental working party. The team, however, only accept this as a 'referral', and the decision to go ahead will not only depend on the team leader's wishes but on whether the use of time is a team priority; a priority determined by:-

(a) the indirect value which may arise for work in the neighbourhood,

(b) what the team has to contribute to the working party,

(c) current pressures on the team, and

(d) how useful would attendance be to the team leader's professional development.

If the decision is in the affirmative, the team leader will be expected to keep to this commitment. In turn all the team will recognise and give time and status to the work entailed. Such a process continually brings out the differential levels of authority existing within departments.

Expanding this to reciprocal relationships between all team members, the essence of 'team-work' can be seen to be in a combination of mutuality and answerability to each other.

The effect of introducing this model for social workers is that the team leader is increasingly seen as a resource and a process is established which clarifies social workers' responsibility for their own professional development Stevenson and Parsloe say, "It may be argued that it is a mark of professionalism in social workers to know their own strengths and weaknesses and to be able to identify when they need help with their work[10]." The team leader, however, remains a manager. Social workers can still expect their individual rights as workers for supervision and direction over policy. Indeed it should be noted that the development of a 'community perspective' (a team understanding of community networks) heightens the knowledge of where the need exists for individual skill development. In addition, the lines of accountability to the department become even more critical as the work of the team becomes increasingly visible. Thus the effect of departmental policy and how it can be influenced become crucial team matters. Finally, responsibility for aspects of conditions of service, such as leave, references, probationary periods and even disciplinary procedures will continue resulting in the retention of some distance between social workers and their team leader.

Underlying the process is a major change in perception, for in addition to the team leader being subject to individual social workers expectations, there are now the team's expectations. The difference is that as a member of the team, the team leader actively contributes to the formation of these expectations. Thus the team as a whole begins to play an integral part in defining the team leader role.

Final Comment

It should be noted that for the changes in expectations described to have any credibility, it is essential that they lie within the team's collective view of meeting the needs of a particular neighbourhood. This can be greatly facilitated if structurally the team takes full responsibility for the work arising from a small defined catchment area. However, I have already mentioned how hard it is to move in a different direction to the established departmental patterns and to swim against the tide, and whatever the structure, a team will still encounter a number of constraints. There will still be elements of competition and rivalry and the team leader will continue to be viewed as spokesman for the team. How the team responds to this situation is central to the likelihood of success in developing an appropriate level of self-determination. When these constraints are combined with the task of changing role relationships within a team, adopting these shifts comes as no easy option with all team members experiencing considerable strain.

The motivation and job satisfaction come from increased feelings of confidence and worth and from the boost inherent in creativity and innovation.

It has been said that the shift in responsibilities described in this paper is tantamount to the team leader shirking responsibility. But this is to misunderstand the nature of the team leader's role in the model that has been outlined. To act in a monitoring, co-ordinating and community development role, to be continually drawing together the different aspects of responsibility accepted by the team and to account for them in terms of team priorities at all levels and to be a good team member is truly a management task.

Note: I wish to express sincere thanks to Anne Vickery for her advice and support in the formation of this paper; and to all sub-office team members, past and present, who have worked so hard in developing this approach.

References

1. Stevenson, O. and Parsloe, P., Social Services Teams: The Practitioners View, H.M.S.O. 1978. Section 13.39. Page 308.
2. Leiserson, A. A Dictionary of the Social Sciences. Editors Gould and Kolb. Tavistock 1964. Page 599.
3. Stevenson, O. and Parsloe, P. Ibid Section 13.60. Page 315.
4. Ibid. Section 13.22. Page 302.
5. Webb, A. L. Co-ordination between Health and Personal Social Services; a question of quality. (Paper given at European Seminar 1975.)
6. Stevenson, O. and Parsloe, P. Ibid Section 14.76. Page 347.
7. Social Services Organisation Research Unit, Brunel Institute of Organisation and Social Studies. Social Services Departments – developing patterns of Work and Organisation, Heinemann, 1974. Page 100.
8. Bennett, B. 'The sub-office; a team approach to local authority fieldwork practice' in Brake, M. and Bailey, R. Radical Social Work Practice, 1980. Edward Arnold. Page 177.
9. Ibid. Page 177.
10. Stevenson, O. and Parsloe, P. Ibid Section 8.94. Page 223.

The Task of the Team Leader:

Relating the Team to the Community

Barry Barnes and John Loughran

"If the social service department is to be geared to its community tasks, then the senior staff . . . will have to demonstrate this community focus in the way in which they carry out their functions within and outside the organization". Seebohm Report[1]

Context

At the time the Seebohm Report was published and implemented there were widespread demands for increased participation in decision making by those who would be affected by the decisions. The consequent reorganization of the social services which took place in this climate allowed innovations to be made. Many followed from questions about the way in which services should be offered to the public.

The practice of social work was touched by these changes. Training courses which had concentrated mainly on psycho-dynamically oriented casework responded by placing more emphasis on a community work approach which was rooted in sociological theory. Students on more social work training courses began to experience teaching from a broader base of social and psychological theory and incorporated these approaches in their subsequent practice.

Similarly the appropriateness of the medical model in the practice of social casework was questioned. The process of investigation, diagnosis and treatment, with its assumption of individual pathology, had been a cornerstone of the casework approach for many years. In this model the client was someone who received treatment *from* a social worker for a problem rather than working together *with* a social worker to resolve the problem. In practice this model was compatible with the traditional hierarchical model of local government departments. These operate on the basis that the communities they serve are passive recipients of a service based on a model which could be depicted in a linear fashion thus:

Department

▼

Team

▼

Community

The Seebohm Committee recommended changes which it hoped would bring about a realignment of the above. The ability of the participants in the three elements of the model to facilitate and promote such a change would influence the success of the new approach. At the same time it was recognised that there would be key people in the new social services departments on whom would fall the responsibility for bonding the realignment. The head of an area based team of workers was one of the people who would have this responsibility.

Team Leader

The structures of social services departments vary one from another. The pattern of internal organisation is significantly different between urban conurbations and rural districts with variations again within each of these.

Whatever the different structures in these departments, there are certain positions within their hierarchies which have this in common, that the person occupying them *has responsibility for leading a team of staff in providing services to a particular community.* Such positions include the District Officer in charge of a large highly differentiated team encompassing a range of sub-groups responsible for providing different services to a community, and a Group Leader in charge of a small group of workers perhaps working from an outposted sub-office. So long as the person has responsibility for leading a team in providing a service to a community then he or she is considered to be a team leader in the context of this chapter.

The amount of delegated authority and the range of services for which the team leader is responsible will differ according to the particular structure and his position within it. Irrespective of this, all team leaders who match our descriptions have to discharge certain common managerial responsibilities.

These responsibilities include identifying need, setting objectives, allocating personnel and resources, monitoring performance, and evaluating the achievement or otherwise of the original objectives. The team leaders' role with respect to both his staff and the services they provide can be considered in terms of these specific responsibilities. Some of these are discussed more fully in other chapters in this book.

Although all of the responsibilities outlined above accrue to each team leader, differing importance and emphasis may be placed on different responsibilities according to political and organisational factors, such as the extent and nature of authority delegated to and by the particular team leader. Consequently, although having a common set of managerial responsibilities, the particular profile will vary from position to position and department to department.

Although this profile is helpful in examining the team leader's job in providing the service or services *to* his community, there is another major factor in this analysis. This is the part played *by* the community itself. At the time of the setting up of social services departments there was no widespread commitment by many local authorities to community participation in decision-making and action. In view of this, the community's own contribution to the provision of services must be an essential factor to be considered by the team leader.

Department – Team – Community: Their Interaction

The interaction between the community, the team and other sections of the department can best be appreciated by looking at the particular transactions taking place. For example, a group of squatters wishing to run a children's playgroup may be negotiating with an essentially administrative section of the department using a community worker in the area office as intermediary.

In this example, the squatters group represents the community, the registration section the department, and the community worker the team – they are all parts of their larger groups and in the context of this particular interaction are seen to be representative of them.

The way the interaction progresses will depend upon the characteristics of the parties involved. Although such a large organisation as a social services department (or a group such as a "community") may be described as having a particular characteristic, it is more helpful to recognise the particular characteristics of their discrete sub-groups and to analyse any interaction in these terms.

In describing organisational characteristics or styles we shall use Blake and Mouton's analysis which they called "The Managerial Grid"[2]. They described styles in terms of the degree of importance given to the performance of the work task as compared with the importance given to the need for good relationships between people. In the example already quoted, the squatters group may attach high importance to both the completion of the task i.e. the registration of the playgroup, and to the maintaining of good relationships with everyone concerned in this negotiation. On the other hand, the registration section in the department may operate on strictly administrative lines, closely following laid-down procedures, and exercising little discretion or flexibility. In terms of work-style, this section would be described as strongly task-, rather than relationship-, oriented. Finally, the community worker may attribute greater importance to maintaining good inter-personal relationships rather than achieving the completion of the task in this case. So, these three positions can be displayed graphically:- as in Figure 1.

Figure 1

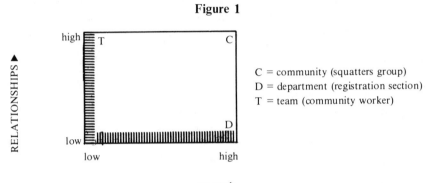

C = community (squatters group)
D = department (registration section)
T = team (community worker)

The community worker is acting as an intermediary between the other two parties. He is also representing the team in this interaction and, therefore, is acting for the team leader insofar as, with the team leaders agreement, he is both representing the team and negotiating across the boundary between the team and other groups. Any team member may hold such a position[3].

In the example already given, no distinction was drawn between the team's style and that of its representative. In many instances, however, there are very obvious differences. For example a local association with whom the team has established a close working relationship wishes to hold a social event. It has sought permission to use the team's staff room. The team members wish for this request to be accepted. Whilst wanting to maintain good links with the association, the team leader has to veto this request for security reasons. This is in keeping with his responsibilities as team leader and is consistent with his view of how he should be relating the team to the community. This contrasts with the team's view which places more importance on the maintenance of good relationships with the community and can be displayed thus:

71

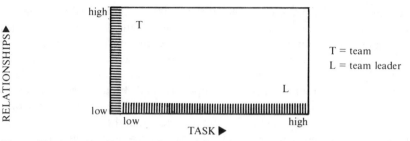

T = team
L = team leader

Team/Community Co-operation

Not only have teams developed differently in their styles, as described above, but also in their responses to, and interaction with, their local communities. These differences between teams have, on the whole, come about as responses to the local variations in the pattern of interaction between the major influences of department/team/community. From a study of these differences, a range of responses emerges which can be portrayed as a continuum based on the team/community relationship. At one end of the continuum, the team dominates the relationship. It initiates, carries out, and evaluates action on the community whose role is very much that of a passive recipient. Traffic is predominantly one way. There is little possibility of and much less capacity for the community to directly effect changes in either the team's structure or style of operation. At the other end of the continuum, the activity is both initiated and executed by the community, and the team plays no part whatever.

At any one time a team may be able to locate itself at several points on this continuum. These will relate both to the range of activities on which it is engaged with the community, and to the different parts of the community with which it is involved. Consequently the particular task of the team leader will vary according to the nature of the activities and where the work lies on the continuum. (See Figure 2 below.) The particular task of the team leader is illustrated in the examples that follow.

Figure 2

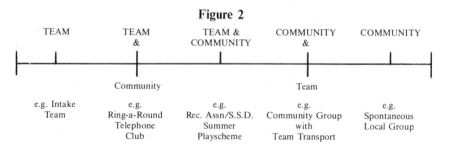

72

For the purpose of illustration, five positions have been identified on this continuum. They will be described together with examples of particular activities which characterise their positions. In the extreme *TEAM only* position, service responses are the sole province of the team, which also identifies the needs to be met, selects the particular need to be tackled, and also allocates the necessary resources. Such an example of a *TEAM only* response is the way an Intake System frequently becomes formalised. The task of the team leader in such a situation can be highly instrumental in encouraging the innovation. In many areas where all social workers participate in a duty rota and also carry a mixed caseload, the pressure of work does not allow for easy communication with the community. The team leader, being in a position to recognise these pressures on the group, can help it to manage the work by bringing about changes in the team's organisation. Such changes as allocating short-term and long-term work to different parts of the team, or the setting up of a permanent duty or intake system are often responses in such situations. Other team leaders have identified particular problems as giving rise to more pressure than others and so have responded by, for example, encouraging special interest groups in the team.

The important element in these activities is that they are conceived and put into practice within the team without seeking community opinion. The assumption is that the team's initiative will in itself result in a better service being provided to the community. This process might be said to represent a traditional local authority response to service provision i.e. the linear department → team → community model referred to earlier in this chapter, where the community remains a passive recipient of the service.

In less prescribed work settings, greater freedom exists for developing new types of relationships with parts of the community. This would be incompatible in a firmly bureaucratic/hierarchical organisation. Often such experiments are very small scale involving the team in working with, and alongside, small parts of the wider community. In the initial stages, the team leader very often has to "give permission" for those members of the team concerned to break away from the usual pattern of interaction with the community. Although there will be a community contribution, there will need to be a very substantial commitment and input from the team, which the team leader must see is maintained for the success of the project and the benefit of the recipients. In addition, it may also be essential for appropriate support to be given by the team to the members of the community engaged in the project, and again it is the team leader's task to ensure that this is provided consistently. An example of such a shared involvement is found in some areas where volunteers have collaborated with local teams in running a telephone club for the disabled. Although there are variations, essentially the team refers clients for the volunteers to telephone at regular intervals and the volunteers are reliant upon the team for ongoing support. In this example the team leader's role is vital in ensuring the team's support for volunteers in the scheme.

Perhaps as a result of this experience, or because of already established traditions, members of the community may take the lead in pointing out unmet needs and suggesting possible responses involving both the team and the community equally. In such a partnership, the team leader has a vital role as negotiator across the team/community boundary, as the maintenance of such an *equal* partnership is a very complex task. Inevitably, the balance of power and influence will sway from one to the other, but it is crucial that an even balance be struck or else the nature of the interaction could return to that of the team predominating with the community feeling deterred from further efforts.

Alternatively, the sway may favour the community, leading to conflicts with the team and having detrimental effects to the joint activity. Naturally such shifts in the balance of influence and involvement will occur. It is very important to maintain the equilibrium by constant dialogue and negotiation between the parties.

This may be done by a team member other than the designated team leader, who then can discharge other important functions. For example, he may be involved as an initial negotiator in working out with a community association and members of his own staff the details of a summer project for handicapped children. The team leader, having satisfactorily completed this part of the task, there would be some advantage in his leaving the responsibility for the day to day running of the scheme to those concerned with it. His role at this stage would become a secondary one in supporting, assessing and evaluating the scheme. To do this, he continues to be a member of the project's committee, through which he provides support to those running the project and influences its direction. In addition, he is able to inform and bring influence to bear in his own department to incorporate the scheme in budgeting, and even in manpower planning. An alternative role might be that of facilitating the scheme by acting as a buffer between it and a departmental structure which may be more indifferent to the scheme than those involved at a team level.

The next stage in the continuum shows *COMMUNITY* being predominant in the partnership. The main prerequisites for this are firstly, a community which is able to produce an individual or group willing to take some formal responsibility for a scheme albeit with the support and encouragement of the team in the initial stages. Secondly, the area team needs to be both receptive to, and supportive of, approaches by the community. The example displayed on the continuum is of a group organised on a weekly basis for local elderly residents who do not want to attend council-run day centres. The ability of the team to arrange transport for the more handicapped members of the group enables it to function and be otherwise independent of council day services for the elderly. At the same time, the health and general condition of members of the group could be monitored through discussion with the group's leaders.

The extreme of the continuum is that service operated independently of the local authority and its social services team. An example of this might be a group of local mothers operating a baby-sitting service to enable each other to complete their weekly shopping. They advertise themselves locally through health clinics and the area office.

Some implications for the Team Leader

The team leader is a member of the management structure in the department representing the views of the central management group to the area team and vice versa. The discomfort in this role arises because the team leader has to represent both groups without alienating one or the other group in his day to day practice. He has a responsibility to communicate area practice to senior management in a way in which the area feels supported and strengthened. In doing so he may need to secure senior management support for a particular approach so as to enable it to continue at an area level. In the process he may even find himself to be challenging established departmental thinking about a particular practice. He may be in an isolated position or may discover that he is expressing views widely held in the department but which have not been articulated. At the same time, he will be expected to carry out committee and departmental policy at an area level. This may require him to draw on similar negotiating and interpretive skills to those which have been used in his contacts with the central management group. His ability to provide an equable service to the community will depend on his ability to balance these two elements of the department – team – community model. In this, he will be expected both to innovate and to support innovations in his team which make for a more effective service.

Paragraph 504 of the Report of the Seebohm Committee states that:-

"the head of the area office will need to see his function as relating the office to the local community as well as providing the established social services and managing its internal organisation"[4].

These three elements and the tension between them form the chief sources of pressure on the team leader in the carrying out of his job. His own style of work will influence his ability to accommodate himself to these pressures. The departmental pressure on the team leader to provide an efficient casework service is a perpetual one. His ability to satisfy departmental management that statutory commitments are being fulfilled will affect his success in establishing more effective team approaches to problem solving in the local community. In doing this, the task is to match community need with departmental resources which include professional social work expertise. The breakdown of the linear department → team → community approach to the service would seem to be the most effective way of sensitising the local authority to a broader-based approach to service provision. The considered dialogue between the community and the team as illustrated by the examples on the central part of the continuum, (Figure 2), we believe, will lead to a more fruitful style of service delivery as envisaged by the Seebohm Report.

References

1. Seebohm, F., Chairman. Report of the Committee on Local Authority and Allied Personal Social Services, Cmd. 3703 July 1968. Para. 502.
2. Blake, R. and Mouton, J. "The Managerial Grid" Gulf Publishing, Horton 1964.
3. For further discussion of leadership as a boundary function controlling transactions between the inside and outside of groups see Miller, E. J. and Rice, S. K. "Systems of Organisation" Tavistock Publications 1967.
4. ibid.

Forward Planning – the team leader's contribution

David Johnston

The purpose of this paper is to outline how a team leader may use forward planning as a useful method to assist him in fulfilling his task. Elsewhere in this book the competing and contradictory demands placed on the team leader by his role in the organisation are discussed. It is all too easy to become immersed in these day to day pressures. The demands of operational problems can easily fill one's time. Forward planning is one method the team leader can use to give a sense of perspective on his work, and by which he can set targets, and evaluate the performance of both himself and his team. My intention is to show how forward planning is relevant, practical and satisfying for the team leader. At the same time I hope to remove some of the mystery and anxiety from the forward planning process.

This paper is organised into five sections, drawing on my own experience and some published work. It begins by defining what I mean by forward planning. There are various very practical issues to which team leaders should address themselves using forward planning methods. I look at how planning can provide teams with a more powerful voice in resource allocation, promote teamwork, improve operational effectiveness and inform workers about their clientele. Next is a long section describing the planning process stage by stage. This method can provide tools essential to identifying the team's objectives; to organising the resources required to fulfil them; and influencing other decision makers. Fourthly I describe an exercise in Warwickshire in which all the area team leaders took part in a forward planning operation. Finally, I bring together some of my ideas in the conclusion.

Why Forward Plan at all? What value does it have for the Team Leader

Writing in the summer of 1981 it may seem to some that forward planning is a luxurious academic exercise. Most of us are too concerned with how we can hold our own in the face of financial stringency to consider any future development. However, I would argue that it is particularly in this situation that some estimate of one's objectives, and therefore of one's priorities is essential. Any decision about resource allocation involves choices, whether in a time of plenty or of scarcity. In the latter situation, however, it is even more vital that we make the best use of the available resources, and we need to be clear about our targets and objectives.

A team leader who wishes to maximize his chances of influencing the distribution of resources needs to maximize his involvement in the planning exercise. Frequently those who 'win' in the resources 'game' are those who are best informed, and able to present a good case at the right time. Forward planning is a continuous process, perhaps carried out as a major formal exercise once a year, but subject to review. Proposals can be made to suit changing political, financial and professional considerations. A team could with some effort make an attempt to influence resource allocation by making proposals for the organisation's budget. This would probably be the largest operation within the scope of most teams. This would, in most circumstances, have to take the form of an inter-team exercise, and later I shall briefly describe Warwickshire's experience.

Forward planning has other uses. It is a vital tool in setting team objectives. One of the team leader's major tasks is to create an atmosphere of participation by team members in order to promote effectiveness. One aspect of management by objectives is the setting of attainable targets for the team. One must identify the needs of the clientele being served, and translate these into the appropriate objectives within the resources available. Teams and tasks differ. A team of probation officers in an inner city faces different challenges to a team of social workers attached to a mental health centre in a new town. The team leader's task has common features in identifying and setting targets for and with the team.

Teams vary in their type, function, size and composition. Despite this, team work is a common goal, but it remains intangible and elusive. Effective teamwork is essential if the tasks of social work are to be carried out. Teamwork has been described[1] as:

1. team members understanding and being committed to team objectives,

2. requiring the maximum utilization of the different resources, skills and knowledge of each member of the team and

3. operating with flexibility and creativity in order to respond to changing situations.

Having identified realistic objectives, this provides the team leader with a method of measuring his team's performance. Forward planning can provide both a framework within which to determine those objectives, and a means of review and evaluation.

Forward planning comes into its own by influencing how the task is defined. *Team Objective setting* in my view is one of the great attractions of the task of the team leader. For all social work teams there is a great potential to choose the method of working and the 'target' groups. As the years pass, one can change the methods and targets as needs and situations change. Social work is a changing scene, with new techniques opening up possibilities of which the team leader will wish to take advantage.

Forward planning can take the form of preparing targets, perhaps an annual list of objectives. These objectives can be reviewed as the year progresses and can be changed as they are achieved, continued with or abandoned altogether as being impractical as the team gives up. A recent list for my own team included amongst others:

1. establish lunch clubs for the elderly,

2. set up 'task force' of children in trouble, to carry out community service projects as an intermediate treatment scheme,

3. start call-in surgery in one high demand village,

4. start work with group of single parents (by one particular social worker),

5. improve liaison over mentally ill in community with G.P.s, etc.

This list was drawn up asking each team member to propose his own list, and the suggestions were correlated at a team meeting. Several of the schemes had been the subject of discussion for some months, and were not new, but the exercise did point up areas of work not covered, and enabled some mild 'brain storming' to take place. Having drawn up the list it became, symbolically, the property of the team, legitimating the work done by an individual member in implementing a scheme.

Forward planning is valuable as a means for a team to get to know the community which it serves. Good planning will involve other departments, organisations, professionals, volunteers, and members of the community. Simply finding out what is going on in one's area of concern can be very fruitful, and lead to one rethinking strategies. I shall discuss some of the techniques of forward planning in the next section, but throughout the process the planner and the clientele (in the widest sense) should be engaged in a continual dialogue. This dialogue can add flesh to the bones of identifying issues, collecting data, choosing strategies, and provide support for implementing proposals.

As well as its practical value, forward planning has an important symbolic value. It enables the team leader to abstract himself from the daily task of allocation, review, supervision and consultation, to take on a *proactive* rather than a reactive stance. This distinction is more highly developed in current debate on police work rather than social work. The issue is whether policemen are best employed 'reacting' to calls to deal with 'trouble' from the public, or should be deployed in the community before 'trouble' occurs. In terms of social work the question can be formulated in whether to respond to referrals, as they come, or examine the demand, in order to identify 'risk' and monitor or meet 'need' before referrals come in. In some teams one hears of a fatalistic attitude to referrals, where it is assumed they come as if by chance and the team has no method of anticipating them. (It is noteworthy how frequently military metaphors are used in the argot of social workers, with talk of 'bombardment rates', and of duty officers being 'in the front line'.)

Put simply, forward planning provides one means of use to a team leader in gaining greater control over his team's workload. Some of the knowledge gained from forward planning can also assist in what is for many the crucial task of the team leader, the operational management of the team. These techniques can help the team leader deploy his staff most effectively. Does the demand presented to the team require a social worker being present throughout the working day? Do situations requiring immediate action create crises in the team in order to find someone available? On the other hand is 'the duty officer' sitting doing little, sitting as it were at the top of the greasy pole waiting for the fire bell to ring? A team leader needs to know when the periods of peak demand are, how frequently emergencies occur and consider these with the main sources of work, the referrers. Other potential issues which can be addressed are whether to use a 'patch' system (currently in vogue), or attachment to G.P.'s or schools, or use workers as specialists.

Forward planning then is as much an attitude of mind as a set of techniques. The method is useful to the team leader, as to any manager, who wishes to maximize control over his team's workload, over the resources available to it, and to minimize the effects of the rather unpredictable nature of the social work task. I shall now go on to describe some of the methods used in forward planning.

The Team Leader's Contribution to Forward Planning

At each stage in forward planning, the team leader can make a specific contribution. I shall describe each stage outlining the necessary steps, and the skills required of the team leader.

1. *Identify Policy Options*

The first task is to identify the policy framework within which the team's work is carried out, and against which any proposals for change will be judged.

The team leader is generally the gate keeper of the team, the member who has most contact with other members of the departmental hierarchy. It falls to him to make himself aware of how the team's ideas are likely to be received. There is no point in presenting recommendations which unknowingly run counter to local committee or departmental policy. Presenting a case to change policy is to be recommended, but an approach which does not acknowledge this is merely naive. He must also make himself aware of the policies of other agencies and how his plans may be affected by them. Frustration can result if a detailed, well-researched piece of work arguing for a new old peoples' home is presented only to discover the Housing Department already has advanced plans for a housing scheme for the elderly in the same place. My earlier point about being aware of what is going on for your clientele is relevant here. You may well find that your concern, say about provision for the under fives on one estate is shared by health visitors, doctors, P.P.A. (even parents), and to propose a strategy using their ideas and support is preferable and more likely to succeed.

Frequently one feels one knows what is required, but in order to influence decision makers one needs to collect data to 'prove' it.

2. *Data Collection by the Team*

Having identified the purpose, the next task is to decide what information is required[2]. 'Hard' data normally refers to quantitative information, sets of statistics, as opposed to 'soft' data which is more based on feelings. Already you have a good deal of 'hard' information available. All statutory social work agencies prepare annual statistics about their work for submission to Central Government. Frequently this is seen as a chore, and the reliability of the figures viewed sceptically (especially if they are produced on the basis of last year's figure plus 5%). Maybe if they were seen to be useful more effort would go into their production! Nevertheless information is available in a form which permits comparisons with other teams within the same authority, and between authorities. It should be possible to use the team's records to tell which parts of the area generate the most demand, who requests help, and of what type. There should also be information on who receives services, for instance, receiving day care for the mentally handicapped. A comparison of the number of people receiving particular services, with the total numbers known in that client group may point up an area of need.

The major sources of information from outside the agency are the Census reports, and population projections available from the local Planning Department. These should be viewed with caution. The Census figures age and they are always out of date when published. Population projections can only be best estimates. The figures should be read against County, District and local Plans of likely changes in the community, planned growth, development of industry and the like.

Part of the task of the team leader in data collection is to use the strength of different team members' knowledge and skills. Home helps may well know more about the problems of some client groups than anyone else. A team leader should seek to involve his whole team in seeking out information.

The collection of *soft* data may involve the team in the most time-consuming part of the exercise, but despite this it can add an essential qualitative dimension. Identifying a phenomenon as a problem requires recognition of it as a situation which is undesirable and needs action to deal with it. Sources of data within the wider community include shopkeepers, clergy, doctors, health visitors, schools, residents and many others. One selects those most relevant to the subject, for instance those who know the needs of parents of handicapped children, are probably the parents themselves. (Rarely do they seem to be asked!) Indeed, in the business we are in frequently the collection of data can be the beginning of problem solving. One study reported that half the people admitted to old people's homes over a given period of time come from the homes of their relatives. These rarely used domiciliary services, and the applicants themselves were less well-known to the department than people living in their own homes. An exercise to identify those people caring for elderly relatives in their own homes, and offering them services is both part of forward planning and problem solving.

A common exercise is to examine the needs of a particular estate, village or ward, which appears to generate a high demand for services.

Merely describing one estate does not demonstrate how it differs from others; it is necessary to compare it with norms for the rest of the team's area, such as the population profile, referral figures, services available[3].

3. *Choice of Objective – Negotiation and Bargaining Skills*
How to meet need can open up further debate. At team level one should aim to identify a number of options (possible solutions requiring different resources) because the process of decision making requires considerable negotiation and bargaining, and ideas which are too rigid may be unsuccessful. In order to discuss this fully I shall describe one example.

The team has identified a large number of handicapped adults, dependent on ageing parents. It is likely that many of them will require some sort of care as their parents grow older and unable to care for them. Four policy options are identified:

1. Hospital care – requiring few resources from the social services department.

2. Use of voluntary trust providing residential care and occupation on one site – with considerable on-going revenue costs for the social services department.

3. Provide hostel – capital and less on-going revenue costs.

4. Group homes with voluntecr help – little capital cost, and less on-going costs.

These options are no doubt proposed in the light of various ideologies and notions of good practice. However at team level rarely does one know fully what resources might be available. In addition each of the options is probably appropriate for some members of the client group, but not for all. Further there is unlikely to be unanimous agreement over what should be done. The interplay of these factors gives scope for a great deal of negotiation and bargaining for which the team leader should be prepared.

The bargaining in this example may go something like this.

The parents of potential recipients may prefer option 2. The professionals with a philosophy of maximising independence would opt for 4. However, option 1. for a period of training, leading to option 4. in the long term may well be the most practical, depending on health service policies, and available resources. It may feel strange to argue for hospitalization, the very regime which one started out wishing to avoid. It is seen as an article of faith in social work to argue for community as opposed to institutional care. Remember though it may not be cheaper if extensive support services, such as day care are required[4]. One has to be prepared to argue the difficult case where it is the more desirable.

Providing choices and alternatives permits one to pick up proposals later as resources change. The team leader, by his position has to accept a good deal of the work of negotiation and skill in bargaining is essential.

4. Presentation
In his position as the team's representative within the organisation, the presentation of the plan needs to be considered by the team leader. Proposals

frequently require approval or resources outside of the control of the team. Presentation (how a proposal looks) is vital to its success. A paper should be easily digestible, not too long and easy to read. Key paragraphs should be readily found, to refer back to later. It is as well to present it in such a way that a reader can find his way easily through the argument.

When writing the team leader needs to bear in mind his audience. Beware of 'teaching your grandmother to suck eggs', but at the same time do not expect the recipient to have to read into your paper assumptions with which you live every day, but of which he may not be aware.

The team leader is also in a position to anticipate the kinds of questions which will be asked of the proposal. Social workers lay great stress on one-to-one, face-to-face communication, but in resource allocation, one's report frequently has to stand alone to argue the case. Delay for further information can be fatal.

Consult those whose agreement and support is required regularly through the tasks of problem definition, data collection and choice, so that actual presentation does not come as a surprise.

Publication can also lead to pitfalls. One should be prepared to brief the press adequately perhaps with a summary paper. The price of mis-reporting can be heavy. The organiser of a club for the elderly may never speak to you again if you announce in the paper that services for the elderly in her area are poor. Make sure she knows what you are going to say, has been involved before you say it, and by that time, supports your arguments.

5. *The Budget – the Team Leader's Timing is Crucial*

This section concentrates on local government. Other agencies have different budget processes and a team leader needs to be aware of the process in his own agency if he is to take advantage of his forward planning.

There is not space, nor am I qualified, to discuss the intricacies of local government finance. In broad outline though the budget process brings together the expenditure required by spending departments and the constraints on resources imposed by the Authority. This latter figure is not solely within the Authority's power to control, being based on three sources of finance, government grant, income from fees, and rates. All three are, in political terms, highly negotiable.

There are three main stages at which bids for resources can be made. The first is the mid-summer preceding the start of the financial year in the following

April. The team's ideas will have to be constructed during the Autumn and Winter prior to that, effectively eighteen months ahead. The outcome of these bids will not be known until February when the resources available, known as the rate precept, are fixed. Local Authorities differ in the formal machinery for this. The second is during the financial year when schemes within the budget estimates can be put up. Some schemes may be put back because it is felt they will take up too great a share of resources. The third strategy is to make an advantage out of the common criticism about local authority finance, spending the surpluses in particular areas of under spending, at the end of the financial year. Often it is felt that this money is squandered on less essential projects, but for the skilful there may be opportunities for projects to be considered, almost as a windfall.

Timing is of crucial importance therefore, and knowing which schemes to put up and when is a mattter of skilled judgement. I would suggest that large schemes involving major resources have to be available at the first stage, but less elaborate schemes can be dealt with later. In a time of scarce resources it is unlikely that 'windfall' projects would succeed if they involved major on-going expenditure. Remember that in schemes involving capital expenditure the major burden is the on-going 'revenue' cost. For instance mini-buses are cheap compared to the costs of fuel, maintenance and the driver's salary.

6. *Competition and its Implications for Teamwork*

The construction and 'sale' of a project through forward planning has several consequences for the work of the team. Where team members are involved in the planning process, the group can become more cohesive, more task oriented, more loyal, and leadership may become more autocratic. Other groups in the organisation, with whom it appears the team are competing, typically 'admin' but possibly 'research' or 'residential' can become viewed as the enemy and only their worst aspects rather than their strengths perceived. At the same time the team may not recognise its own weaknesses and blot out anything that does not support its own position. 'Winning' or 'losing' can exacerbate these tendencies. In a similar way to political parties after losing elections, less effective teamwork can be the result. 'Winning' can lead to improved work, but can lead to complacency. 'Losing' can lead to inter-group fighting, but if focussed positively, also to the group learning more about itself, and re-examining its functioning. A team leader must ensure that the emotional energy put into a project, does not become all consuming. It is tempting for a new team leader to latch on to a scheme in order to put right an acute problem as perceived by the team. This can lead to a high degree of team cohesion, but he must ensure that inter-action and communication continue with other teams in the organisation and that the objectives requiring co-operation with them are also sought. Resource bargaining, and its inevitable competitiveness has advantages for team work, but it does have attendant risks.

Area Development Plans – The Warwickshire Experience

A brief description follows of an exercise carried out in my own Authority to prepare Area Development Plans for the whole county, during the winter of 1978/79. The task was to write a development plan for the period 1980–1985. The area officers, who were then team leaders, had been meeting together for some years making suggestions and recommendations on departmental policy on a piece meal, issue by issue basis. It became clear that each area officer was ignorant about the area teams other than his own; that each was generally unaware of the differences in workload, management, pressures of demand, and team responses over the county. As a result their individual proposals were rather idiosyncratic and open to criticism. Warwickshire Area Officers have two main functions, the first is to manage the resources of their area team, including residential, day, domiciliary and fieldwork services and the second is a community development role including liaison with voluntary organisations, promoting local initiatives and the like. The Area Plans covered both aspects, but emphasized the latter.

The preparation of the Plans took place within the framework of a training exercise. We involved staff from other sections of our own department, e.g. finance and research, but also from outside, such as Planning, Secretary's and Treasurers' Departments Work tying into their own planning systems, and ex-ploring general issues around budgeting and finance were carried out with key personnel from these departments. The training exercise took place on one day each month for six months. The plans had to be completed by March, as a specific aim was to make a contribution to the department's bid for the 1980/81 budget, which had to be finalised by May[5].

In most area teams the writing of the Plan, though the responsibi-lity of the area officer was undertaken by the whole team. Individual members took charge of particular aspects, maybe on services for a particular client group. Various sources of data were possible, but most plans concentrated on what was close at hand – their own annual statistics, and information on caseloads and referrals. In some plans the police were involved over juveniles in trouble, and the Department of Health and Social Security over the number of single parent families. Sometimes figures were available over a period of time. When over four or five years, it was possible to describe trends.

To make comparison easier, a standard format was agreed as shown below, and more or less adhered to by the authors.

1. Geographical description.

2. Demographic description.

3. Team structure and organisation, intake and service delivery.

4. Services and establishments already available.

5. Allied services.

6. Development proposals.

7. Implications for resources.

8. Summary of recommendations.

9. Statistical appendix

The section on implications for resources was interesting and sobering, involving estimating the cost of facilities. The recommendations were less firm as they looked further into the future.

All through the writing phase we were conscious of the major task beyond the production of the plans, how to 'sell' them to higher management. This was done in several ways. Individually area officers discussed their plans with their own line superiors. Some of the key personnel in finance and research had been involved in the training programme, and the group of area officers met with the director. We were helped by the presence of the deputy director throughout the training exercise and deliberations. This process of consultation culminated in the group writing of a joint paper (on one side of A.4) to the departmental management team at its budget meeting. We had to swallow our local interests and identify our common problems. It also showed how changes in one area affected another, permitting a common approach. Although our recommendations were not accepted as a whole, many of our ideas were accepted, and there is always next year!

We also learnt lessons. We found we lacked data on mental handicap and mental illness, and on some other department's planning, e.g. District Councils and the Department of Employment. On the other hand, data was readily available on children, the elderly and the handicapped. The plans also showed unrecognised differences in the nature of teams in rural and urban areas and how 'objective' methods of resource allocation, such as home help hours by proportion of the population aged over 75 can become out of date, and not reflect local conditions, such as availability of day care.

Overall the exercise was of great value. Area Officers were better informed about their own areas, and had been able to consider how well their resources were deployed. They also knew more about how similar problems were tackled in other area teams. There is now a bank of data which can be drawn on in future negotiations about resources. It is intended that the plans shall be up-dated each year, in order to present other joint papers on resources, for each year's budget process.

CONCLUSIONS: The Team Leader's Task

In this paper I have argued that the use of forward planning can assist the team leader in making sense of the unpredictable and potentially contradictory nature of his task. A team leader to manage his team effectively needs to maximize the control the team can exercise over the work load.

Forward planning is a continuous exercise essential to good team work. Though there is a lot of mystique attached to 'research', all team leaders should involve themselves in exercises to inform themselves better of their task and to review their use of resources. Some may say this is a counsel of perfection; fine if *you* have the time but *I* am busy. I would argue that it is only by some sort of forward planning exercise that one will be able to 'helicopter' – to lift oneself out of the day to day hurly-burly. If team leaders are not prepared to find the time to reflect on what they are doing, they are condemning themselves and their teams to merely 'reacting' to whatever demands are made of them. They will never be in control.

Much of the skill a team leader needs to master is basic to good social work practice. The effective worker needs to set himself objectives, and evaluate his performance, and this is true of effective forward planning. In addition the skills of report writing and presentation are similar in principle to other reports used in social work practice, and skills learned in advocacy will be useful in bargaining and negotiation.

For forward planning to be effective, the team leader needs to use all his management skills, involving his team in a common problem-solving exercise. Good forward planning is dependent upon a style which promotes the effective use of all the resources, especially of manpower, available to the team leader.

References

1. Marsh, N. Huddersfield Polytechnic, unpublished paper.
2. See Glampson, A., Scott, T., Thomas, D. N.: *A Guide to the assessment of community needs and resources.* NISW 1975.
3. See May, J. *Health and Social Services Journal.* 24.6.77.
4. Armitage, M. "The Cost of Caring for the Elderly", *Social Work Today.* 5.6.79.
5. For experience from another Authority see Anderson, D. "Enabling practitioners to contribute to practice", *Social Work Today.* 12.6.79.

Task Allocation and Workload Management
Colin Hardy

The team leader is in a key position to influence both practice and policy. If better services are to be provided within finite resources, team leaders may need to consider their management style and move towards a more systematic approach to task allocation and workload management.

There has been a wealth of written material concerning the identification of priorities and the management of workloads. I doubt there is a definitive model as many agencies develop variations on a theme in response to their own particular needs, and this is the case in my own experience since 1974.

Using published work from the National Institute for Social Work and Brunel University, I joined with three other members of the area staff to develop another system. We had been specifically given the brief to produce a team based workload management system with the capacity to both manage individual cases as well as the total team's workload, and a system which could reflect a chosen sequence of priorities and activities represented in an area policy.

We felt that many of the existing systems were descriptive rather than prescriptive and had become particularly complex in the way in which they identified work and reflected responses to demand.

Our overall objective was to provide some direction in the area's work which could be stated and measured against known criteria and altered in the light of experience. Within this, each team should be given a clear and specific brief in which individual workers would function effectively.

The view was adopted that if the social worker was freed from unproductive anxiety not only about the work for which he had responsibility, but also for work which he could not take on, better performance could be expected. The anxieties relating to service refusal particularly and more generally to the level of service offered, should appropriately rest with the team leader and his reference group at area management. Whatever one's views of social worker autonomy it did not seem reasonable to expect the practitioner to be making fundamental choices of priority or direction for the agency. Nor did we feel it reasonable for the team leader to continue to allocate work without formal recognition of the worker's time and skills required to achieve worthwhile results.

The system was required also to be able to provide a framework in which specific tasks could be identified and managed, within the context of the worker's total workload, the team's workload and area policy. Traditionally, the supervision process often fails to place an emphasis on prescribing not only the priority to be given to individual pieces of work but also the method which may be effectively employed. For the team leader an ability was called for to allocate tasks to individuals and to generate a complementary team effort where some choice of skills and preference may be developed.

Clearly, in order to be able to manage work at either team level or individual case level, there must exist a clear way of identifying it. Similarly, if one is then wishing to make a statement about what response one gives to that work demand, then an agreed form of describing service delivery must also be developed. The purpose of our development of a "client problems" dictionary and an "interventions" dictionary was to be able firstly to provide a position statement and secondly, to state an intent in terms of client problems, resources and the allocation of the agencies' response.

The client problems dictionary employs three levels of severity for each of six client groupings. The intervention dictionary lists five levels of activity and the location. (Appendix A and B).

It is important in recognising the total work demand which exists within the team to be able to identify areas of resource generation and other activities which cannot be specifically related to individual clients but nonetheless are accepted parts of the social worker workload. Included therefore in the client problems dictionary are descriptive statements of resource and liaison tasks.

In the developmental phase of using the problems dictionary and interventions dictionary, it is clearly necessary to be able to arrive at a concensus of what constitutes, for example, the most severe elderly case or the least severe physically handicapped case. Contrary to our own anxieties, such agreement was not difficult to at least a reasonable degree of accuracy. During this process social workers will need to be able to reflect their own value systems in terms of, for example, whether one has an individualistic base to client problem codings (such as the one attached at Appendix A), or whether to make a move towards a more collective statement about client need. Whichever form is adopted, the team should be clear that it reflects their style of work in terms of their understanding of the social problems within

91

their area and the type of methods that they may employ as social workers to respond to perceived demand.

I would not encourage any team leader to adopt a ready made system with all its descriptive tools unless he and his colleagues sincerely feel that it does reflect their value systems and working ethos.

Having then identified the work and the range of possible responses to it, it is necessary to look at the management of the individual social worker's activities. The team leader as allocator needs a clear framework in which to function and the area therefore must ensure that it is in a position to be able to make some statements of relativity as between client groups. The agency itself should state the value placed on work with one group of clients as opposed to another. Similarly, the effort in respect of resource generation needs to be fully integrated into such statements. The traditional way in which these priorities can be stated is in an area ranking sequence which lists all the agencies' client problems and resource activities in descending order of priority, see Appendix C.

During the process of arriving at such a ranking sequence, the agency will need to resolve whether for example, it chooses to offer a better service to fewer clients or for example a reduced service to a greater number of clients. Similarly, the staff involved will need to express their choice concerning for example, crisis work versus the need to develop preventive community support networks.

Whatever the overall policy directions of the agency, individual social workers require sufficient time in relation to agreed activities to be able to achieve specific results. The workload management system must focus on the allocation of time to tasks.

Again, as with work identity and priority systems there are a great many possible variations. In order to achieve our objective of implementing a management tool with specificity, we arranged the allocation of hours to tasks on a monthly basis. Dependent on the style of work adopted by teams the planning period of a month could be varied but I would doubt that it would be desirable to seek to reduce the planning period to less than a week or more than six or eight weeks. The difficulty in reducing the planning period to a shorter one would be that the process of identifying work and allocating time to it would need to take place more regularly; conversely, if the planning period is too long, one may lose the sense of being task-specific when planning work.

The process of managing the social workers workload begins with identifying the total amount of time available. This can be simply calculated as being the total number of working days during the planning period (per month) multiplied by the number of hours per day. For a full time worker this will commonly fall in the range 160 to 180 hours per month.

Social workers appear to spend time in connection with two main areas of activities. These can be described as variable and non-variable. The non-variable activities are fully listed in Appendix D and include responsibilities towards day duty, supervision given and received, team meetings, leave, training etc. Each worker should be able to identify at the beginning of each planning cycle, the amount of time to be allocated to these non-case responsibilities. By agreeing time to be allocated and subtracting from the total amount available, a period of time available for case type activities is identified. In practice it is not uncommon to find that many social workers deploy over a third of their total time to matters which do not bear directly on their particular clients.

The purpose of identifying these blocks of time is clearly to achieve some control over them. The team leader will need to decide whether or not it is acceptable for the worker to be spending time in the way he is. The team leader will need to consider whether a particular social worker should have more time available for case type responsibilities by decreasing obligations to, for example, day duty. Similarly, the team leader will need to consider the impact on case objectives of the worker being absent on, (for example) legitimate training courses.

Having then identified the period of time available for case type activities, it is necessary to list the total current work load under this heading. (See Appendix E). In doing so, one must ensure that not only are individual cases and case components listed but also any responsibility the worker may have for example, for group work or resource generation. If a worker is responsible for working with a group then it should be an acknowledged part of his workload and compete for time with other responsibilities. Only in this way will development work or alternatives to casework be identified, valued and preserved at times of crisis. Many workers do complain that when they are "under pressure", tasks such as foster parent enquiries are left because they make less demands and consequently achieve a lower priority, and plans in respect of long term cases are shelved because of the more immediate demands from newly allocated work. These anxieties (or lack of controls)

93

appear to stem largely from under-management of the workload and a lack of an agreed order of priorities.

In looking at the individual cases, the team leader will need to consider to what extent each case may have a number of work generators within it. For example, a family with two children in residential care and a further child in a foster home could be considered to be three separate generators of work, each requiring a different yet co-ordinated response. It cannot be assumed that the objectives for one part of the family harmonise with objectives being set for other case components. Consequently, it is necessary to break each case down into task areas and to consider the relative priority between them during the process of allocating time.

The team leader and social worker must agree on an overall plan for each piece of work and a commitment to certain activities in the specified period. Furthermore, a level of agreement is required as to what constitutes case or activity time. If this is seen as meaning time spent travelling to the client, recording, interviews, telephone calls, visits, case conferences etc., then each activity must be allocated time to achieve specified aims. (See Appendix F). Negotiation between a worker and team leader must be realistic for it may be found that a relatively simple task requires large amounts of time. For example, with review in a community home school out of area, the travelling time alone may be several hours. Add to this, preparation of the review itself and interviews with key figures and the total time commitment may be very high. Social workers tend to underestimate the amount of time required to complete various pieces of work and the team leader as work controller must establish himself in a clear position to be able to approve or disapprove of activities because of the time they take.

It will be necessary for the team leader and the social worker to go through each piece of case type work and identify tasks and allocate time to them. Having done so for the entire workload, clearly some comparison between the commitment and the time available to achieve that commitment is required. If the worker is under-committed, then the team leader can either agree to extending case objectives or use the time by allocating further pieces of work. Similarly, if the worker is over-committed, the team leader must consider whether to limit individual case objectives and to reduce the time spent or reduce the total workload. During this debate the team leader must consider whether any periods of time need to be left unallocated so that the worker can pick up work later in the month. This will be particularly relevant, for example, in an intake team where the turnover of work is greater and there will be some acknowledgement of the amount of work to be allocated as the planning period progress.

It should be stressed that the purpose of this approach to management is not to reduce professional autonomy or to over-manage but to enable. Good management should be seen as a pre-requisite to good practice. With any negotiation between worker and team leader, not only must the worker press for time to undertake pieces of work but the team leader should begin to direct as to how time is spent. Critics may argue that a professional social worker will order his own time and that his autonomy must be preserved. How then is a group of workers described as a team able to plan, co-ordinate and evaluate their individual efforts to the greatest effect? The relationship between the worker and the team leader in this management approach dictates a sharing which may be absent from supervision in its more usual form; in exchange for protection from over-allocation offered by the team leader, the worker considers giving up some independence of action. The team leader will find himself more aware of individual workers' skills and preferences in allocating not only cases but tasks within cases. Recognition will be made of worker skills, thus more time may be required by one worker to undertake tasks which another worker, because of his level of experience and skill, finds less time consuming.

The degree to which the team leader involves himself in method prescription and task identification will vary and may take place within normal "supervision" as opposed to the work planning session. The work planning contact should not be used for case supervision. If debate is required as to the case characteristics and the style of work required this should be discussed in supervision sessions. It should be the clarity of that supervision which is brought to the work-planning stage.

With experience it should be possible, in approximately an hour, to plan work for the coming month and agree specific tasks, but considerable discipline on the part of both the worker and the team leader will be required.

This style of management may identify for the team leader the skills and methods available in the team in a more precise way and should open the way for encouraging workers to develop skills or acquire others. Teams not uncommonly function in a highly individualistic fashion which results in the team leader holding the only overall understanding about his team's functioning. This may be far from satisfactory and have the effect of under-valuing workers' efforts by preventing acknowledgement. The information base provided by employing workload management systems however can be very influential in helping the team leader to establish a shared team approach. The team leader will be able to identify factors such as total work loads, the nature of problems and their severity, and should be informed about work flow patterns, work preference and skills in a much more specific way. By relating these factors to the area's overall priorities and the specific brief which may be given to a particular team, the team leader and the team as a whole has before it a range of alternatives. The extent to which the team leader has autonomy within the area may vary, but the team can be in a position to pool its own resources and develop its own alternatives in terms of deployment of time and skills.

The amount of administrative back-up needed for a team based workload management system is not great and it is desirable to place administration of the system with the team leader (to avoid team members viewing this management tool as a bureaucratic chore). Appendices D and E provide workload record sheets on which the various phases of the system are reflected in terms of the time committed to agreed activities. The team leader may quite properly accept responsibility for maintaining these records during the work planning session and subsequently will be in a position to summate his team's activities and produce an accurate statement about the position of his team.

In doing so, the team leader develops some real bargaining power in relation to other teams as does the area in relation to other areas. It becomes possible to consider the parity of service between teams or to justify imbalance.

The team leader's role is a complex and often conflicting one. It includes responsibility for standards of service and delivery via supervision; supervision itself includes components such as staff development, training, innovating working methods and selection of methods. The team leader is responsible for work allocation and maintaining the standards of work as well as implementing and influencing policy. All these tasks are achieved by a variety of rational and irrational processes with varying degrees of success. Area priority ranking and team based workload management should, however, provide a more rational basis from which to function. No system can provide all answers but the one described encourages the purposeful analysis of demand and response which can result in more explicit decision making and practice. As the client has a right to know what level of service he can expect, so the social worker has a right to be clear as to what the expectations are regarding his involvement with clients or more generally in relation to his other responsibilities. We should remind ourselves that good team leadership is quite properly to manage and direct individual and team effort into profitable and effective tasks. The decision to offer a service and the extent and style of that service is primarily the team leader's in relation to area policy and good practice. The practitioner's role is perhaps to negotiate with the team leader the work objectives and the methods and tasks and to implement the decision reached. The burden of work which the agency cannot carry out should not be passed on to the practitioner but should be managed by a policy of priorities at team and area level. This style of work may well pose a serious challenge to traditional team leader/practitioner relationships. In seeking to provide effective services, this challenge should be faced professionally with good management seen as a pre-requisite to good practice.

APPENDIX A   SOCIAL PROBLEMS AND RESOURCE DICTIONARY
PROBLEM DEFINITION

CLIENT GROUPS			
CHILDREN	C1 Grossly disturbed emotional or social functioning, significant abuse, seriously inadequate care.	C2 Seriously disturbed emotional or social functioning. Inadequate care.	C3 Occasional evidence of minor disturbance in emotional or social functioning. Marginal care.
ELDERLY	E1 Grossly ill with major social dysfunction. Very dependent with seriously inadequate support available.	E2 Severely ill with some crisis in social functioning. Inadequate support available.	E3 Occasional illness with some problems in social functioning. Marginal support available.
FAMILY	F1 Gross social, emotional, financial dysfunction within family unit and in its external relations.	F2 Severe social, emotional, financial dysfunction within family unit and in its external relations.	F3 Some evidence of, or occasional social, emotional financial dysfunction within family unit and in its external relations.
MENTALLY HANDICAPPED	MH1 Grossly handicapped with major social dysfunction. Seriously inadequate support available.	MH2 Severely handicapped with some crisis in social functioning. Inadequate support available.	MH3 Minor handicap with occasional problems in social functioning. Marginal support available.
MENTALLY ILL	MI1 Acute mental ill health with major social dysfunction. Uncontainable in Community.	MI2 Severe mental illness with some crisis in social functioning. Inadequate support available.	MI3 Occasional minor mental illness with some problems of social functioning. Marginal support available.
PHYSICALLY HANDICAPPED	P1 Grossly handicapped occasioning major social dysfunction. Seriously inadequate support available.	P2 Severe handicap with some crisis in social functioning. Inadequate support available.	P3 Minor handicap with some problems in social functioning. Marginal support available.

RESOURCES

HOMEFINDING — (1) Adoptive Homes, recruitment and approval. (2) Guardian - ad - litem. (3) Foster Home recruitment, Approval, Supervision. (4) Lodging Schemes.

CHILDMINDERS AND PLAYGROUPS — (1) Childminder Recruitment and Approval. (2) Childminder Development and Supervision. (3) Playgroup Registration and Inspection.

VOLUNTEERS — (1) Recruitment and Approval. (2) Development and Supervision.

COMMUNITY AND GROUP (1) Client Group Development and Supervision. (2) Client Group — Liaison only. (3) Community Group Development. (4) Community Group Liaison.

LIAISON — (1) Liaison with Agencies or Services

APPENDIX B

INTERVENTIONS DICTIONARY

Level 1. Full professional assessment. Allocate for Agency activities responding to immediate crisis and preventing further deterioration.
Intend to achieve sufficient change to enable less intensive Agency activities.

Level 2. Allocate for Agency activities intended to achieve change and preventing further deterioration. Limited assessment, practical services orientation.

Level 3. Action to supply practical services only.

Level 4. Allocate for maintenance, monitoring visits only as time permits.

Level 5. Duty response only.

APPENDIX C

PRIORITY RANKING SEQUENCE

Problem/Resource Area In Priority Order		Level of Service
C1	Homefinding 1 — 4	Level 1
M1	C & P 1.3.	
F1		
E1		
PH1		
MH1		
C2	V 1,2	Level 2
E2	Group and Community 1.3	
F2		
MI2		
MH2		
C3		Level 3
E3		
F3		
PH2		
PH3		
MH3		
MI3		

All Client and Resources at Service Level 3	Level 4

C + P 2
Liaison 1
Group and Community 2 + 4

All Client Groups at Level 3	Level 5

100

APPENDIX D

NON-CASE TIME

HOURS PER MONTH

DATE OF ASSESSMENT	*JAN. 82*
(A) TOTAL TIME AVAILABLE	*172 HRS./MONTH*
NON-CASE COMMITMENT	
Supervision	*4 HRS.*
Day Duty	*30 (4 x 7½)*
Team/Area Meetings	*2*
Leave in Bank Holidays	*–*
Training Given/Received	*–*
Student Supervision	*10 (Weekly x 2½ hr.)*
Liaison Responsibility	*–*
Other Non-Case	*–*
(B) TOTAL	*46*
Time available for Case Projects (A - B)	*172 – 46* *126*
Time committed to Case Project etc. from over	*150 HRS.*
	24 HRS. THIS MONTH OVER-COMMITTED.

101

APPENDIX E

WORKER SUMMARY SHEET

SOCIAL WORKER

CLIENT NAME/PROJECT/GROUP	JAN. 82 DATE REVIEWED CASE CATEGORY TIME ALLOCATION	DATE REVIEWED CASE CATEGORY TIME ALLOCATION	DATE REVIEWED CASE CATEGORY TIME ALLOCATION
ABLE FAMILY *ABLE JOHN*	*F1 – 8 hrs.* *C1 – 20 hrs.*		
I. T. GROUP	*G1 – 20 hrs.*		

TOTAL TIME COMMITTED

TO CLIENTS/PROJECT   *SAY 150*

HOURS PER MONTH

APPENDIX F
IDENTIFYING CASE COMPONENTS

What constitutes the case —

How many components — list them

A. *ABLE FAMILY*
B. *JOHN ABLE*
C.
D.

What is your overall plan with each —

State them

A. *ACCEPTANCE OF JOHN'S ADOPTION*
B. *PREPARATION FOR ADOPTIVE PLACEMENT*
B.
D.

What are you aiming to do this coming month — what method?

State: A. *FAMILY CONTACT RE-REALITY OF FAMILY LIFE + JOHN'S NEEDS.*

B. *CONTINUE LIFE STORY BOOK PLUS CONTACT WITH ADOPTION AGENCY.*

	Hours/Month			
	A.	B.	C.	D.
How many visits — who to — how long —	4	10		
Office appointments —	1			
Contact with other Agencies —		4		
Case Conference or Review —				
Court Attendance —				
Recording inc. Court, C/C, file etc. —	1	2		
Travelling —	2	4		
Phone Calls —				
Anything else including speculating client demand outside that planned for —				
TOTAL for this piece of work	8	20		

The Need for Working Agreements: Social Workers' Expectations of Their Team Leaders in Supervision
Stephen Nixon

Introduction

This chapter examines social workers' expectations of their supervisors in the supervisory process, which is defined below. It reports some of the findings of a pilot study of staff supervision in a social services department office in a Midlands industrial town.

The supervision actually experienced by social workers is contrasted with what they would ideally like to receive. Some elements of the style adopted by supervisors and the expectations concerning content are also described.

The findings indicated a lack of congruence in several areas between the social workers' ideal and the actual current practice. This lack of congruence suggests a need for greater openness between social workers and supervisors.

Such openness might be achieved by means of a contract or working agreement between social workers and staff supervisors. In this way mutual expectations and perceptions could be examined and mutual rights and responsibilities clarified.

Expectations in Supervision

'Supervision' in social work refers to the process of consultation about cases and methods of work but in this chapter it is also assumed to involve the checking or monitoring of work by someone in a senior position, the supervisor[1]. The supervisory process includes therefore opportunities for the discussion of work, professional development, and general support. It also has elements of accountability and control; the supervisor, in a social services department, being responsible for ensuring that work is being done to the best possible standard.

Supervision is just one element of the team leader's task although it is the crucial one in which fieldworker and team leader come into very close contact. There are various general expectations which fieldworkers have as team members[2, 3, 4] but there is also an array of expectations which are more specific and relate to the supervisory relationship and process.

The size of the organisation and the management's attitudes are likely to be crucial to the overall environment in which the supervisory relationship occurs. The individual team leader is almost invariably a member of the area management group. The responsibilities which he has as a manager, his own attitudes and personal interpretations of management also form part of the background to supervision.

Some of the influences upon the fieldworkers' (and the supervisors') expectations are likely to be based on their own early experience of supervision whether as a student, trainee, or upon newly joining a department. The individual's philosophy and approach to social work and the value he places upon supervision are also likely to be crucial; whether he values supervision and sees it as an essential element of professional work or more as a management tool for the control and surveillance of employees.

These varying influences and expectations exist at the point of arrival of the social worker. He brings with him some expectations of the organisation within which he is going to work. The supervisor also has his own expectations and beliefs about his role.

The arrival of the social worker, or his transfer from another area or team is a critical point. The attitude of the supervisor at this stage is vital together with his willingness to discuss his own attitudes and expectations and to listen to the fieldworkers' views. As there are likely to be variations in the expectations of each side and there may be misconceptions, the willingness to discuss these is likely to be an important influence of the pattern of the supervision process for some time.

MacGuffie et al[5] studied the changing interpersonal perceptions of social work supervisors and their student supervisees over a period of a year and found a growing congruence in perception. The interactions between them towards the end of the year were based on developed communalities in perception which tended to minimise the chance of distorted communications and to clarify both cognitions and feelings of communicators. However, the growing congruence in perception was achieved only after intensive interaction over the year and the authors considered that positive attempts should be made to improve the mutual perceptions.

Thus the establishment of a good working relationship as rapidly as possible may be essential if tasks are to be focussed upon and worked at with the minimum of misunderstanding and delay. Mutual expectations and perceptions may differ and when this happens, purposeful communication between the fieldworker and his supervisor may be reduced with consequential results on the effectiveness of both. The establishment of working relationships is discussed later in this chapter.

Pilot Study

In order to study mutual perceptions and expectations in supervision, a research study was undertaken. This chapter reports some of the findings of a small pilot study in a decentralised area office in an urban setting with three social work teams and their leaders. The response rate to the questionnaire was just over two-thirds: fifteen being returned from twenty-two fieldworkers and two from the three team leaders.

The fieldworkers in this study consisted of five men and ten women. Nine were aged under 30 and six were over 40 years of age. Eleven were professionally trained and eight of these had less than three years experience after qualifying. Three others had been qualified for more than four years.

Although the sample and results represent only a small fraction of social work supervision, some of the findings and their implications are interesting and, I think, worthy of consideration.

The study aimed to examine the supervision received by social workers looking at both the quantity and quality, the sort of relationships between the two parties, the supervisor's style and also the content of supervision sessions. In some questions the respondents were asked to indicate how their present actual supervision varied from the sort of supervision they would ideally like to have.

The questionnaire was largely pre-coded, with questions having multiple choice answer boxes to tick. The attitude questions were answered on a five point scale. The possible answers had been drawn up partly after reviewing the literature and partly after several sessions on the subject with a group of non-participant qualified social workers and experienced supervisors.

The Supervisor's Style

To obtain some indication of the supervisor's style, fieldworkers were asked to respond to questions consisting of a series of contrasting elements. These elements were developed from an early study of social work supervision in an American Public Welfare Office[6] but were modified during discussions with the planning group. Some overlap was inherent in certain of the elements, but the aim was to generate an index so that an overall impression could be obtained of supervisors' styles, which could then be compared with other factors in the study.

When asked for their views on what style their supervisors should adopt in an ideal supervisory situation compared with the actual situation at present, the ideal and actual were congruent in respect of several factors. Given contrasting elements along a scale, (relaxed-formal, friendly-detached, readily-not readily available), the social workers indicated most frequently that their current supervisors were 'fairly' relaxed (where 'fairly' is the second point on the five point scale), 'fairly' friendly and 'fairly' readily available. Their ideal supervisors would also be fairly relaxed, fairly friendly and fairly readily available. In these three areas therefore, the social workers expectations were being met.

However, there were other areas where the ideal and actual were not congruent (see Figure 1). The social workers expected that the supervisor should not allow them to work on their own quite as much as they were in actual practice allowed to do. Similarly, the social workers tended to think the supervisor should give more specific instructions than he was doing in current practice. The ideal supervisor was also expected to be more firm in his approach, whereas the supervisors were seen as tending to be more easy-going in practice. Kavanagh's[7] respondents (although not from a social work setting) also indicated the importance of 'structuring behaviour' by the supervisor in order to successfully execute their job responsibilities.

Figure 1: Fieldworker' Reports of Current and Ideal Supervisors' Styles

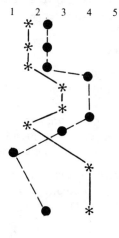

———— ideal							———— current
	1	2	3	4	5		
a. relaxed							formal
b. friendly							detached
c. readily available							available only at formal supervision
d. supervises closely							allows to work on own
e. gives specific instructions							no specific instructions
f. firm							easy going
g. stays in agency rules							goes outside agency rules
h. sees things from agency viewpoint							sees things from client's viewpoint

The social workers also wanted their supervisor to be more willing to go outside the agency rules than they were currently. This linked with another element where the social workers' ideal was a supervisor who gave more consideration to the client's viewpoint than supervisors did in current practice.

The supervisors' views were very similar in all categories, with a major exception: they did not see themselves as needing to give more consideration to the client's view. There appears to be a slight contradiction here with the social workers asking for generally firmer supervision but also hoping that supervisors would consider the client's viewpoint and be more willing to go outside agency rules. However, the desire for firmer supervision is in terms of the structure of the supervision itself rather than in holding them more to agency requirements. It does, nevertheless, point to an important issue. Supervisors have to attempt to combine the interests of the client and those of the agency and, as mentioned above, they themselves expressed no major difficulties in doing so. The social workers however, were certainly asking for a stronger client, rather than agency, orientation, seeing the balance between agency and client as an issue, contrasting with the supervisors' view.

Supervisors felt they were committed to their position and task as supervisors, but lacked confidence in the breadth of their expertise. The social workers indicated their lack of confidence in their supervisors' breadth of knowledge. Indeed, the supervisors' experience was certainly limited, having had fairly minimal experience of social work (2 – 3 years) before being promoted. They indicated their own lack of training for the job of supervisor as well as their lack of experience of supervising students before becoming staff supervisors. The supervisors also reported a lack of confidence in the breadth of their experience and knowledge.

Use Made of Supervisory Sessions

A further comparison was made of the way the social workers used their current supervisory sessions and how they would, in an ideal situation, like to use such sessions. The method used was to give a list of ten activities and topics with a five point scale for each answer indicating levels of importance, usefulness and frequency of use, and in addition, the social workers' perception of the importance given to the various areas by his supervisor.

The items which were selected by the social workers with consistently high frequency were, as might be expected, case consultation and discussion of newly allocated cases, (see Table 1).

These were then followed in level of frequency by discussion of agency and of community resources. It is interesting to note here that social workers put agency resources higher than community resources, but they saw the supervisor stressing community resources rather than agency resources. However, the supervisors in fact claimed that they put agency resources above external community resources.

There would seem to be several implications of this finding.

Table 1: Content of Supervision

Fieldworkers' Ranking Current Content	Variations of Ideal from Current Practice	Fieldworkers' Perceptions of Supervisors' Emphasis	Supervisors' Own Views
Case Consultation			
New Allocation			
Agency Resources		fieldworkers perceive these as reversed for supervisors	
Community Resources			
S.W. Theories			supervisors place these three at top of their list
Practice Skills			
Dept. Policies		seen as higher priority	
Checking/Monitoring	low ideal; higher in current practice	supervisors seen as not stressing this	given low priority by supervisors
Morale Maintenance	low, but seen as very useful	seen as being given a high priority	given high priority
Personal Support	very low	very low	

Supervision is seen, after discussion of cases in case consultation and allocation, as a way of obtaining resources. The supervisor is seen clearly as a 'gate-keeper' in resource allocation.

In addition, the way supervisors are perceived as putting community resources as more important seems to indicate that the supervisor might suggest, in the first instance, the use of resources other than those of the department if at all possible.

Supervision is seen partly as a way of obtaining resources and inevitably there are problems associated with this potentially inadequate way of resource allocation which also has implications for the way clients sometimes receive an inadequate service. Indeed some social workers mentioned that the supervisor acted as the first link in a chain for obtaining certain departmental resources. Direct contact with resource-holders further up the hierarchy was seen as an alternative way of obtaining the resources. Thus informal links and relationships presented the possibility of resource-allocation being determined by informal means without the supervisor being fully involved in the process. It is necessary to obtain a balance between the need for a flexible and speedy response with the possibility of inappropriate or unfair allocation and the more fair but possibly more time-consuming official departmental procedure. A further issue is raised here. Clients certainly detect this restriction in the use of agency resources and feel they are told to look elsewhere.

Two further topics were the discussion of relevant theories and consideration of practice skills. The theories relevant to social work, both from social work literature and from other subject areas were not seen as major areas for discussion in supervision. Similarly, discussion of precise skills used in practice, such as interviewing techniques, were ranked as less important by the social workers. The supervisors were also perceived as giving low priority to these two items. However, in the supervisors' eyes, social work theory and practice were seen as being very important, more so than case consultation and allocation.

The management aspects of the supervisor's role also formed part of this section. Social workers rated the discussion of departmental policies fairly low in their own priorities, but did see their supervisors as giving it a higher importance. That is, they expect supervisors to emphasize departmental policy in supervision sessions. In fact this is where perceptions are congruent, with supervisors stressing department policies very much.

Another area concerned the checking that work is being done to a satisfactory standard, ensuring that records were being kept, decisions adhered to and any statutory requirements being met. The social workers see such checking as having a low priority in an ideal situation, but as having a higher priority in the current practice of supervision. This perhaps indicates the social workers' desire to achieve a professional independence of action, yet recognising that the current organisation of social work within a social services department demands a system of inspection. There is equally the possibility that they also want to share both the responsibility and accountability for work being done. However, an important feature was that social workers saw their supervisors as not stressing this item at all – it came bottom of the rank ordering. (The supervisors themselves gave checking a low priority.) Supervisors are seen as relegating this to the least important of their tasks, but supervisors do need to know how work is being done to ensure that staff development can occur and to avoid poor quality work if at all possible.

The maintenance of morale is often seen as an important role of the supervisor, and the supervisors in this study confirmed the high level of importance they attached to morale boosting. Similarly, the social workers perceived their supervisors as giving this a high priority, expecting them to boost their morale when there are difficulties in the work context and to encourage them in their work generally. From the social workers' own perspective of what they themselves see as important, morale boosting comes very much at a low level in both the actual usage reported and in an ideal situation. However, when asked how useful this morale boosting function had been, some social workers rated it highly. Thus, this seems to indicate that although social workers claim not to use their supervisors for this function very much, some find it very useful when they do, and, in any case, morale boosting is a major expectation that social workers have of their supervisors.

A related factor was whether the social workers would use their supervisors for personal support concerning their own life and problems and this produced the highest frequency of a "not at all important" response. This item produced strong feelings among many of the social workers, a large proportion indicating that this was not part of a supervisor's function.

The various factors reported here appear to be contradictory in the way they are given differing emphases. What emerges is an apparent contradiction in the social workers' attitudes to the supervisor's role. Case consultation and discussion of newly allocated cases were classified as being very important, but items concerning management e.g. discussion of departmental policies, came low down in the list. Checking was seen as important in practice, although played down by the supervisor.

This might appear to be a wish to focus on the more 'professional' aspects of work rather than upon the management aspects. However, there is a further contrast in attitudes in the way discussion of practice skills and relevant theories both come low down in the expectations of social workers and their perceptions of supervisors.

Effectiveness of Supervision
Another series of questions was concerned with the effectiveness of supervision. In order to assess effectiveness, one has to consider how far the goals of supervision have been met. Clearly there is every likelihood that the

effectiveness of supervision will be viewed differently by different individuals in varying posts within a department; the director's expectations will diverge considerably from those of a fieldworker. Even if the general outlook to 'professional social work', for example, is similar, the balance between the varying elements of effectiveness is likely to be different.

Thus in trying to ascertain effectiveness, we have to consider the aspects of quality of service to clients, the professional development of the worker, the meeting of agency objectives through the fieldworkers and the adequacy of support offered to the fieldworker. Hence there is a whole array of aspects contained within 'effectiveness' which have to be considered and some assessment made of the standard achieved and the contribution of supervision to this.

Responses to the questions on effectiveness showed some disparities between social workers' and supervisors' views (see Figure 2). Notably, social workers said they had learned about the agency, whereas supervisors had put this lower down the list.

Figure 2: Effectiveness of Supervision: Fieldworkers' and Supervisors' Views

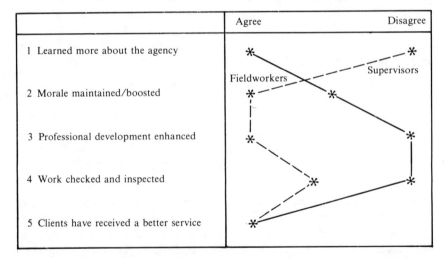

Social workers also saw morale as having been moderately maintained, whereas supervisors thought this had been particularly effective. In addition, supervisors considered the professional development of social workers had been enhanced, but social workers reported that this was the least effective aspect.

Supervisors thought that the checking was moderately effective, but social workers felt this to be less effective. However, both fieldworkers and supervisors agreed that the clients had had a better service with, rather than without, supervision.

Implications

The various discrepancies in expectations between social workers and supervisors and the lack of congruence between the social workers' ideal and the actual supervision received appear to be linked with the dissatisfaction with supervision which was expressed by more than half the social workers. Fuller discussion of mutual expectations and the bases of supervision might provide an opportunity to close the gap between the ideal and the actual, thus increasing satisfaction with supervision.

Contracts in social work are a well established part of Reid's task-centred system[8] and Pincus and Minahan[9] devoted an entire chapter to the issues involved in negotiating contracts. Sheldon has also discussed the use of contracts in social work practice[10]. Recently, contracts have been adapted to social work education in both the student-tutor relationship[11] and student-fieldwork teacher-tutor relationships[12,13,] The writers have claimed various benefits from the introduction of such contracts including the greater clarity of purpose, improvement in planning of placements, detecting where difficulties arose more quickly, involving the students in devising their own educational goals and decreasing discontent on placements.

These benefits claimed for the use of contracts in social work education, although largely based on the subjective assessments of the authors rather than upon any objective monitoring, seem worthy of note. This is particularly so if the findings reported in the first part of this chapter concerning the lack of congruence between the expectations and the actuality of supervision are a common feature of supervision. Adopting a form of more open relationship between supervisor and supervisee may help to improve the supervisory process and ultimately, service to the client.

There are of course differences in the aims of contract-making in direct social work practice and in social work education, as well as in working agreements between supervisors and social workers. The' aims in direct practice contracts are to try to improve in some way the client's well-being and his situation. In social work education, the contract's aim is basically to secure improved learning opportunities for the student; the contract is mainly to help the student as an end in itself. A working agreement between supervisor and social worker would aim to improve the service delivery to clients, ensuring that social work skills were used to the best advantage and providing an opportunity for staff development for that particular social worker. Similar aims were suggested by Fox[14].

Contracts or Working Agreements in Staff Supervision

In this next part a discussion follows about the possible place in staff supervision of the idea of a contract, or working agreement, between the supervisor and the social worker. The use of contracts in social work practice in general and in social work education in particular will be considered. Some of the advantages and likely problems which could arise in trying to evolve and use such working agreements will be examined.

There is a danger of misconstruing the word 'contract' in the present context and a brief explanation of the use of the word is important. The word 'contract' has strong legalistic connotations and therefore is of dubious use in a social work setting which needs more flexibility than the binding restrictions that a legal contract implies. Rimmer[15] has drawn attention to the dangers of borrowing words and phrases which have clear meaning outside social work jargon. She has specifically discussed the problems involved with the term, contract. Recently Corden has explored in a discussion of Contract Law, the issues on introducing a contractual model into social work practice[16]. The term 'contract' already appears to have an established place in social work, for example, Pincus and Minahan's use of the word. However, as the use of the word contract is open to misinterpretation, particularly in the context of staff supervision, it is perhaps wise to avoid using it unless the intended meaning is clearly defined.

Pincus and Minahan discuss the term contract, also providing an alternative phrase 'working agreement' which seems to be less ambiguous. Their definition is "the worker needs to establish at least a temporary working agreement which defines the nature of his relationship with the other persons, the goals and methods and the responsibilities of each party. The terms of the contract as well as commitment to it, may be implicit or explicit".[17] Therefore, during this present discussion although the word contract will occur from time to time, the meaning to be attached to it is no more than that of a 'working agreement'.

Already there exists in any working relationship an implicit or sometimes an explicit contract, but not necessarily of the sort to improve supervisory practice and outcome[18].

Blau and Scott[19] in discussing supervisory relationships point out that the authority of supervisors in a formal organisation is legitimated by legal contract. Thus the social worker in a social services department is an employee who is under a contractual obligation to follow managerial objectives. Supervisors and supervisees have their own job descriptions which will indicate to some extent the authority of the supervisor over the supervisee. In social work this is modified perhaps by the professional, or semi-professional elements, which guide the social workers' activities, but inevitably a supervisor is a superior in the organisational context.

The potential here for professional versus bureaucratic conflict has been much discussed[20] but is an important element to bear in mind in a consideration of working agreements. The supervisor is without doubt in a formal position of power over the social worker whether or not he has professional authority in social work terms; the social worker is accountable to his team leader for the work he does.

Establishing Working Agreements

When establishing an initial relationship, people bring many expectations which are derived from various sources. These include previous experiences with other supervisors or social workers, their experiences in similar or different agencies, the hearsay evidence about the person concerned and their observations and any stereotyping which takes place in their minds. At a first meeting, certain behaviour will be expected and the person will collect data to confirm or repudiate their expectations.

It would therefore be advantageous if these expectations existing at the start of the supervisory relationship could be brought out into the open, thus establishing a working agreement from the very start on the basis of mutually discussed and agreed (perhaps agreeing to differ) expectations of each other and of the supervision process[21].

The purpose of a working agreement between supervisor and social worker would have to be clarified, including such broad aims as the provision of good service to clients and the development of the social worker's knowledge and skills. The *terms* of the working agreement would also need to be elaborated. These would include the types of goals, the tasks each would perform, the techniques to be used, differing values, limitations of knowledge and skill, lack of resources, the constraints of agency policy and the requirements of working agreements established with other people e.g. consultants or other social workers in the team. The roles of the participants would need to be discussed so that the expectations of each concerning their respective contributions were clear and finally, the responsibilities and obligations of each side delineated.

Such clarification would serve several purposes. For example, it would help to indicate what would and would not occur, to forestall false expectations, and to help each side to determine how to accomplish objectives.

Characteristics of Working Agreements

In discussing contracts in direct social work practice, Seabury[22] has described four major characteristics and these would be essential to any working agreement in staff supervision.

(1) The agreement should be *explicit* in order to reduce misunderstandings and frustrating interactions because such confusion and hostility may occur if one party does not follow through what the other thought was an *implied* term of the agreement. Such an agreement would be fully accepted only when each person does actually meet at the agreed time and place and fulfill their part of the agreement. Without such commitment any working agreement would be rather hollow.

(2) The working agreement should be *mutually agreed* with the terms understandable and both parties approving its provisions.

(3) The working agreement should be *dynamic and flexible* so it must be renegotiated when thought necessary because no working agreement can cover all contingencies which may occur over a period of time.

(4) It is important that the agreement should be *realistic and equitable* and that any responsibilities and goals should be within the capacities of each side.

The process of negotiating a working agreement would go through different stages of development, becoming more specific and better understood as the agreement continued. A first phase would be exploration, when each side shares their expectations and come to a joint understanding about their obligations and purpose. This would then develop into a tentative agreement despite uncertainties and reservations. Following this a primary working agreement could be established when both parties have reached mutual and explicit understanding of the goals and procedures, and the terms are clear and accepted.

The existence of secondary working agreements is an important consideration as these would involve the supervisor in working agreements with other team members and consultants. Thus, for example, the frequency

116

of interruptions is a major complaint of social workers about supervision sessions. However, an attempt to establish sessions free from interruptions has to be balanced against the importance of availability to other team members with whom working agreements concerning availability might be negotiated.

Renegotiation of working agreements would be essential from time to time. One contingency that might have to be handled is the fact that some supervisors, perhaps promoted early in a time of rapid expansion, do not have the requisite breadth of knowledge and expertise. Indeed as fieldworkers develop their skills and expertise there is every likelihood of them seeking the most appropriate source of knowledge or opportunities for discussion with someone whose judgement is valued and trusted. This could occur in team sessions where the team as a whole acts as a supervisory resource but is equally likely to be sought more informally through contact with peers, other supervisors and departmental specialists or consultants. The worker should be able to turn to the most appropriate person without going outside a working agreement. The closed nature of some supervisory relationships may need to be renegotiated and made more open to allow a more flexible use of the most appropriate resource.

Negotiation of working agreements would involve, for example, the regular negotiation of agendas for supervision sessions. The content of supervision is as vital as the relationship between the two parties involved.

Thus there would need to be discussion of the areas of skill and knowledge which are required by the fieldworker concerned i.e. establishing of goals and tasks. The inevitability that supervision is time-limited would require that sessions were pre-planned and focussed on particular subjects which could be explored. Other similar cases could be allocated to that worker to increase his expertise in that particular area. The usefulness of 'off-the-cuff' discussions is likely to be of more limited value than those where both participants have devoted some time and thought to preparation.

Staff development is therefore an important element within supervision as it is through more experienced and skilled social workers that improved service to clients can be made possible.

The Advantages and Limitations of Working Agreements

A lack of planning is possibly a major characteristic in much current supervision, and this was certainly apparent in the pilot study. Thus a working agreement could be used to improve the planning and value of

117

supervision sessions. Indeed, there could be a link between the lack of purposefulness in some social work practice and the lack of planning and purposefulness in social work supervision. If supervision sessions, which are very much under the control of social worker and team leader, are not planned, there is the possibility that this may be reflected in a similar lack of planning in direct work with clients.

A working agreement could be useful in examining the focus of supervision on tasks and areas of learning. Indeed a working agreement is implicit in all relationships. The negotiation of a working agreement is a deliberate and conscious articulation and shaping of the informal working agreements that are inherent in all relationships, into a form that will facilitate the attainment of goals established[24].

An initial working agreement might provide a base line with which to evaluate the supervision and the progress made during the period under consideration. It might also be useful in considering accountability and responsibilities because such matters would be discussed and clarified at an early stage. Working agreements should enable each party to have a greater awareness of each other and enable a greater participation by the social worker in the supervisory process. The social worker might be able to emerge from being a passive recipient (or is it perhaps the supervisor who is the passive recipient?) to an active participant within a known framework. It might also lessen the problems of covert or double agendas in supervision. The negotiation of a working agreement would give each the shared experience of exploring the issues involved, immediate involvement, mutual commitment and readiness to assume responsibilities[25].

The negotiation of a working relationship is really a way of establishing a meaningful relationship as rapidly as possible, so that the tasks can be focussed upon and worked upon with the minimum of misunderstanding and delay.

Limitations

There are however, limitations in the establishment and use of working agreements. They are an idea difficult to put into action. For example, as several people are involved in any team it would be necessary to negotiate with all concerned, establishing different working agreements with each. There would almost inevitably be some conflict over the range of different agreements, if only because of the limitations of time and resources.

The current system of very varying and flexible supervision arrangements might be lost with a more formalized negotiation of working agreements and this could lead to inflexibility in supervisory arrangements. In addition, there might be some danger of higher management attempting to use working agreements between supervisors and social workers as a way of exercising more control over social workers.

There is also the danger that once a working agreement has been established, it might become fixed and inflexible in operation by either supervisor or social worker. It would be essential to avoid this and regular renegotiation of working agreements would be an important element.

However, this in itself raises further unintended consequences; there could be so much discussion of the working agreement that it might become the focus of work rather than the means of achieving a better outcome. Linked to this there is the problem that there would be a focus on the business side of supervision and there might be a loss of balance with the relationship element. Indeed the emphasis on negotiating working agreements in this way may make supervision relationships rather mechanistic, moving too far away from the important element of support which must remain a key factor in supervision. Social work is now predominantly a job being done in large scale organisations where the efficient use of manpower is essential. However, it is important to be aware of, and concerned about, the individual worker (or supervisor) so that his efforts are noticed and support is available to him.

This discussion has concentrated upon the supervisory relationship between supervisor and social worker. However, the supervisor has numerous other responsibilities which take up his time, for example, area management meetings, administrative duties concerned with the running of the team, consideration of allocation of new work, preparation for supervision sessions and reading files and reports. In addition, the supervisor has responsibilities for liaising with external bodies and may have a caseload of his or her own. Social workers have expectations about their team leaders with regard to these activities which are an important part of running a team. However, such activities are less visible to the social worker and limit the supervisor's availability for supervision sessions and consultation at times of crisis. Maintaining a balance between these various activities and availability to team members is an important task of the team leader.

Conclusions

The social workers' views reported here indicate some varying expectations in the role of the supervisor. Social workers approach supervision with priorities and expectations which are at variance with those of their supervisors. There is the danger that these differing expectations are not discussed and openly acknowledged. Social worker and supervisor may misunderstand each other, sometimes be uncertain of the purposes, and misinterpret the aims and actions of the other. There is thus a risk of poor communication in supervision, yet effective communication is so essential in the practice of supervision in social work. The social worker is only likely to raise matters which he sees as relevant and regarded as such by his supervisor. The social worker must have an accurate knowledge of the supervisor and his attitudes and equally, it is important that the supervisor must be aware of the social worker's perceptions of him.

This brief study shows that there seems to be a lack of agreement about the functions of staff supervision. If it is to fulfil any functions adequately it is important that mutual expectations are clearly expressed. Such knowledge and awareness and the necessary relationship cannot be built up overnight. It is difficult to achieve this without the necessary explanations and discussions of roles, functions and attitudes. A working agreement must be established between the supervisor and the supervisee, and should be explicit. There has to be an open discussion of matters such as what supervision is, how the social worker is expected to use it and equally what the social worker would like to achieve through supervision. The managerial element is perhaps that most emphasized in many supervision situations, but many social workers regret the lack of opportunity to discuss professional matters. Without trying to suggest that there ought to be a standardised working agreement between supervisor and social worker, it would appear to be desirable that each side knows how the other is operating; that the individual requirements of the social worker are tailored to the right supervisor so that when they discuss work, the expectations and messages are being understood and interpreted correctly.

Besides the development and use of working agreements, it might be possible to match the social worker and supervisor. To achieve this, it would be important to allow some flexibility in the creation of teams and subsequent allocation of new workers. Discussion of working agreements between supervisors and fieldworkers could occur before a final commitment and changes permitted without embarrassment or penalty. In addition, mention has already been made of the informal arrangements which fieldworkers make to meet their need for opportunities to discuss their work. This raises the issue of maintaining accountability. When social workers reach a high level of skilled professional work and seek out the best opportunities for consultations with the most appropriate sources, existing patterns of supervision may have to be redesigned.

References

1. Parsloe, P. & Hill, M. (1978) in Stevenson, O. and Parsloe, P. Social Services Teams: The Practitioner's View. HMSO.
2. Gutridge, P. (1974) in Management in the Social Services – The Team Leader's Task. ed. R. Olsen. UCN Wales Bangor.
3. Bennett, Bill (chapter in this book).
4. Pettes, D. (1979) Staff and Student Supervision: a task centred approach. G. Allen and Unwin.
5. MacGuffie, R. A., Janzen, F. V. & McPhee, W. M. (1970) The Expression and Perception of Feelings Between Students and Supervisors in a Practicum Setting. Counsellor Education and Supervision 10, pp 263 – 71.
6. Blau and Scott (1963) Formal Organisations. p. 140. Routledge and Kegan Paul.
7. Kavanagh, M. J. (1975) Expected Supervisory Behaviour, Interpersonal Trust and Environmental Preferences. Organisational Behaviour and Human Performance, Vol. 13, pp 17 – 30.
8. Reid, W. J. (1978) The Task Centred System. Columbia.
9. Pincus, A. & Minahan, A. (1973) Social Work Practice: Model and Method. Peacock Publishers.
10. Sheldon, B. (1980) The Use of Contracts in Social Work Practice. BASW.
11. Parsloe, P. The Use of "Contracts" on a Social Work Course, in "Trends in Social Work Education". ed. O. Stevenson, ATSWE Working Paper 2.
12. Parsloe, P. (op. cit.).
13. Robinson, M. Contract making in social work practice: An experiment in social work education. In "Trends in Social Work Education", ed. O. Stevenson, ATSWE Working Paper 2.
14. Fox, R. (1974) Supervision by Contract. Social Casework, April 1974, pp 247 – 251.
15. Rimmer, J. (1978) "Contract" and other Interlopers in Social Work, in "The Unitary Model" ed. R. Olsen, BASW.
16. Corden, J. (1980) Contracts in Social Work Practice. BJSW, Vol. 10, No. 12, pp 143 – 161.
17. Pincus, A. & Minahan, A. (1973) op. cit. p. 93.
18. Stiles, E. (1963) "Supervision in Practice" Social Casework, Vol. 44, January, pp 19 – 25.
19. Blau, P. M. & Scott, W. R. (1963) op. cit.
20. Toren, N. (1972) Social Work: The Case of a Semi Profession. Sage Publications.
21. Pettes, D. op. cit. p. 62.
22. Seabury, B. A. (1976) The Contract: uses, abuses and limitations. Social Work U.S.A., January, Vol. 21, No. 1, pp 16 – 21.
23. Pettes, D. op. cit. Chapter 6.
24. Pincus, A. & Minahan, A. (1977) A Model for Social Work Practice, in Specht, H. & Vickery, A. Integrating Social Work Methods. G. Allen and Unwin.
25. Maluccio, A. N. & Marlow, W. D. (1974) The Case for Contract. Social Work U.S.A., January, Vol. 19, No. 1, pp 28 – 37.

Staff Development in the Team

Malcolm Payne

Introduction

This chapter is divided into two parts. The first contains a discussion of a number of general and conceptual issues about staff development which a team leader might consider. It discusses why staff development can be seen as an important aspect of the team leader's role, and various aspects of its definition.

The second and longer part discusses some practical ways in which the team leader can involve his team and its members in successful staff development.

Issues in staff development

Why Staff Development?

The responsibility for staff development often seems to sit uneasily with other managerial and leadership roles. It seems to require different skills and resources from other managerial tasks and it looks to the future, so its impact on the team and the individuals in it may be uncertain. All this means that it may be fitted in when more important things do not command the team's attention, or be simply a matter of allowing members of the team to attend courses as they wish.

In fact, staff development, in a broad sense, is a constant preoccupation of teams and their leaders. Individuals are usually concerned with their personal development; members of work groups are usually concerned about the relationships between colleagues and improvement in the value of the work they do; team leaders are concerned to enhance the effectiveness of the group that is the instrument of the work they manage and the individuals who undertake that work.

Team leaders in their managerial role, therefore, have a direct concern with staff development because their job as a manager is to get the work of the agency done well. Staff development is a way to help the team to achieve a greater level of ability in doing their work. The need for observing, controlling and directing by the manager is partly replaced by self-evaluation, self-control and self-direction along the lines of the agency's policy, by a more able and more autonomous worker.

There is a distinction between development of individuals within the team and development of the team as a group. Both are necessary and complementary to one another. As individuals make progress in their personal development they change in their relationships with work colleagues. As the team changes, this affects how individuals function within it and how they see their future. This can lead to a problem in that development of one individual in one direction may be seen to have deleterious effects on the development of others in that direction or elsewhere. It may also lead to gains in that individuals and teams are part of each other so that the team may help develop individuals within it, and individuals can stimulate change in the team. Although, as has been argued, his management responsibility includes staff development and the team leader may be seen as one of the most important of those individuals, he should not take the whole responsibility. This is, in part, because a major aspect of the development of individuals and groups is taking responsibility for progress. Staff must therefore be involved in all good staff development. Another point is that leadership and management roles do not mean that the leader has to control or manage all changes, but that he may also stimulate others to act and offer permission for creative action by others. Since the leader cannot know everything that team members need and want in their personal and group development their involvement in identifying and meeting these is clearly needed. Staff development, therefore, must be seen in the context of group as well as individual development. The team, the individual and the role of the leader are the three main elements in staff development and will be considered in this chapter together. Some aspects of staff development obviously involve more of a personal focus than a group focus and more or less of the team leader, but each of the three elements is always present.

The meaning of staff development

There are a number of difficulties about the meaning of development which lead to confusion when planning, and uncertainty in implementation of, staff development.

Since social work involves the social worker in building and using relationships with people in the community, competence as a social worker depends on both technical ability to carry out procedures and the way the social worker uses his personal attributes. Therefore, the social worker's development may (not necessarily will) depend on change in his personality and attitudes as well as improvement in his skills and knowledge. This raises ethical difficulties for someone concerned with staff development particularly if he is the worker's superior in a hierarchical system of management. The involvement of a representative of the worker's employer in his personal values and attitudes may prove unacceptable, particularly if there is an implication of personality assessment. If managers' involvement in personal assessments of workers is misunderstood, the way may be opened to conflicts of principle being interpreted by powerful superiors as defects in the worker's personal capacity. Such assessments may then get caught up in power conflicts within the agency.

There are two ways out of these difficulties: safeguards and a clear understanding of what is meant by personal development. Appropriate safeguards might limit personal evaluations to self-evaluations or evaluations by equal colleagues. Evaluations related to work matters might be linked directly to evidence from items of the worker's practice about which interpretations are agreed by the worker. Any documents which are written could be kept by those being evaluated and not subject to report to higher authority. It should also be clear whether any inadequacies being identified are inadequacies in the basic competence to do the job, or are inadequacies when compared with a higher standard of competence. Opportunities to make an evaluation of the evaluator may also help.

Nevertheless, a *definition* of development which clarifies what activities and behaviour are seen as developments, and provides a clear terminology for such evaluations, is necessary.

'Development' is used rather indiscriminately to describe situations in which improvements or approved events occur. It connotes, therefore, a situation in which something gets better. This view aligns with Meyer's statement that the goal of staff development is that "practice is improved, the policies and progress of the agency are carried out more effectively and its clients are better serviced[1]." Development is an evaluative concept, and it is necessary to be clear about who makes the evaluation. The subjects of the development, either individual members of staff or the team as a group should clearly feel that an improvement has taken place. So the team leader in his role as representative of the agency management and staff would consider as an important factor in their evaluation, whether clients are better served.

There are a number of different emphases which might be placed on the *process* of staff development. One approach is that of Briggs[2] who views staff development as an 'administrative process' consisting of "getting things done by influencing staff activity and *decision making* to work towards attainment of agency objectives". (italics original). He sees staff development as a way of getting formal goals agreed in the agency implemented by influencing staff from within their own value system rather than imposing requirements by use of hierarchial power. An alternative emphasis is assumed by Pettes[3] who views staff development as concerned primarily with education:

"The teaching role of the team leader comes to the fore in relation to his responsibility for staff development . . . The gap between what the worker knows and what he needs to know defines the area of the supervisor's teaching responsibilities".

In her discussion, applications of power by the agency are seen as an aid in the educative process:

". . . we will examine how evaluation of staff may be used as an aid to teaching and learning".

A more comprehensive view is taken by Thomas and Warburton[4] discussing staff development among community workers in social services departments. They describe it as 'monitoring, and helping to enhance the quality of work'. The process is seen as a systematic 'ordering of experiences' so that learning can take place. They argue that community workers avoid critical or controlling influences in their contacts with others and so

". . . are not exposed to any systematic influence which can monitor, assess and guide their activities".

Another factor emphasised by Cohen[5] is the importance of work experience as an essential element:

"Overall, such programs strive to effect growth and change in professional performance as a result of the work experience in a particular setting."

This is emphasised by Briggs[6] who argues that in-service education which is part of staff development should involve "*inductive learning* moving from the specific to the general" (original italics) rather than teaching general principles and deriving specific applications from them.

Drawing on the elements proposed by these writers, staff development may be conceived as a process in which an agency, as represented by a manager with responsibility for the work of a group of staff makes decisions about objectives which its staff should fulfil. The staff should then be involved in a process of monitoring and evaluating their work and education towards organising the knowledge, skills and attitudes gained from their work in ways which guide their activities along lines which seem to the agency and the staff concerned to provide a better service for the clients and community they serve. This may eventually involve changes in the original objectives.

Finally, it is helpful to examine the criteria by which judgements can be made about whether 'development' has taken place: the *objectives* of development. The need to prevent unreasonably subjective judgements about workers and derive the improvement directly from work experience requires the objectives to be defined concretely rather than as generalised aims or ideals for progress. Several groups of factors are evident in the elements of staff development considered above.

First, the team, collectively and individually will have to *monitor and evaluate* their work. They make fuller, clearer and more accurate descriptions of what they are doing in relation to client groups and communities and explain more fully how that description relates to the objectives that are set by the agency and by themselves. What assumptions underlie their work in this instance, including value assumptions, and what skills they have used in carrying out their work can also be clarified. The first stage of development, then, is a clearer and more sophisticated description of work.

The second stage is to make judgements about the work described based on the objectives, assumptions, knowledge and skills described. This is the stage of making explicit *evaluations* and arguing for them using the evidence of the events which have taken place.

The third stage is to make *generalisations* and *orderings* of the information and evaluations already devised. If more generalisations can be made, or a greater number of different events linked, or events ordered for the first time or reordered in a way which seems to make more sense, then development has taken place.

The fourth stage is *setting new objectives* and *testing* actions in practice which derive from the new generalisations which have arisen. At this stage, actual changes in practice can be seen and it is only then that the development can be described as *secured*. In their turn, secured developments lead to a new cycle of development, perhaps building on the previous development or on a new area.

Summary

This section on the meaning of staff development has argued that it is a concept which implies an improvement in social work competence. The improvement must be seen as such by both staff and representatives of the agency policy-makers, and include changes in the ability and personality of the worker. The improvement takes place through a process in which representatives of the agency set objectives, involving staff in monitoring and evaluating their work towards organising their knowledge, skills and attitudes in different ways which meet the objectives or require that new objectives be set. The objectives should relate to the community and clients served. The improvement is jointly evaluated by seeking explicit evidence of the improvement of descriptions of social work activity leading to evaluation of work, new generalisations about knowledge and experience, setting and establishing new objectives and changed methods of undertaking the work.

The Practice of Staff Development

Starting points

There has to be a starting point for the involvement of team members with the team leader in staff development and this occurs when both the activity and their involvement is made explicit: for individuals, as Nixon[7] suggests, an explicit decision by written contract or open discussion helps to create the firmer supervision and clear objectives most workers seem to want. The team leader needs to make a clear decision to give organised attention to this aspect of his work. Time should be set aside for the thought, planning and administration involved and in supervision sessions and team meetings to start the process. Unless this is done, staff development in the early stages is always taken over by other more pressing direct work with clients. As a programme gets underway the amount of time involved may need to be controlled in the other direction, lest it take over the whole time of the team.

Making a starting point with the team is more difficult. A group decision to start staff development should be taken freely and one of the problems facing a team leader is how to introduce the possibilities without damaging future involvement by seeming to impose a decision. Even the relatively light commitment implied by introducing the topic may be enough to create unwilling agreement among some team members, who will afterwards destroy any progress by their lack of involvement. On the other hand, not everyone will want their work patterns disturbed by development and some may need to be pressed at first. If they are pressed by their peers rather than the team leader it may secure at least lack of obstructiveness, and prevent resentment arising over the feeling that the agency has applied pressure.

There are many starting points in the life of any team which can also form the starting point of staff development activities. When a new member of staff comes, for instance, suggesting that the team devise a programme for his induction this may raise issues about the work the team does, the community it services, the organisation of the team and methods of presenting them to an outsider and achieving his involvement in it.

The start of any new project or activity involves looking at the skills, knowledge and attitudes required to carry it out effectively and how those may be gained within the team. Leydendecker[7] identifies other crucial points at which a staff development programme can usefully be introduced, such as when new social work methods are to be introduced; when learning opportunities are made for recently qualified staff to learn specialised knowledge which cannot be made available on a basic training course; preparing staff to work with ancillary staff or volunteers; and preparing staff for administrative or educational roles.

Often the issue of starting a staff development programme is raised by members of the team. This opportunity to explore the issues without the lead coming from the leader should be carefully seized. Sometimes such moves come from newly-trained members of the team, frustrated by an apparently stable, changeless team, from someone with a clear change in mind using staff development as an instrument for change, or from someone who see 'staff development' as 'in-service training' and does not see the full implications for individuals and the team as a whole. Unless the team has a chance to explore without commitment what they might gain and lose from the exercise, these individuals may find themselves in a difficult relationship with other members and the hidden motives may create conflicts which destroy the programme.

The present position

Once a staff development programme is accepted by the team some kind of assessment of the present position must be made in order to plan where staff want to develop to.

One way of doing this is to have an individual session with each member of the team to decide on an appropriate programme for him and amalgamate the individual programmes to form (where there are similar needs) shared activities. This has the advantage of clearly recognising and working to individual needs and carrying out what may be a delicate exercise in private and in an existing and, it is to be hoped, strong relationship. There are, however, disadvantages. Such a method does not test the differences between members of the team on each other and members are not enabled to take into account the direction others are taking. It individualises the process, so that group strength in the team is not enhanced and the opportunity is lost for team direction to emerge as well as an aggregate of individual directions. The personal evaluation is carried out in private with a person in authority over the social worker and this may inhibit the accuracy and completeness of the evaluation. There is also the risk of biasing judgements in the direction of the leader's view, however tentatively he conducts the interview. This approach also means that individuals do not take responsibility for themselves and their teams and that slows the development of teamwork. Sometimes issues cannot be thoroughly explored when there are only two contributors to a complex discussion and finally an individualised scheme makes it difficult for the team to include its leader in its development: the implication is that he does not need development in the same way and as part of the process. Admittedly staff development planning is more complicated and difficult to do in the group, but that only reflects the complexity and difficulty of the task. A team exercise, however, raises the problem of controlling and stimulating such an exercise. A group discussion does not provide enough structure, and team leaders may be unsure about running other possibilities.

A programme has to enable both individuals and the team to examine that part of their past which is relevant to their work, their present activities and their future needs. One way of doing so is to carry out a *self-positioning exercise*. A similar programme is used at Bristol University to enable social work students to examine their experience and needs and plan their courses[9]. It is derived from the work of Priestley *et al*[10] with prisoners, young offenders and other clients, and also works well with social workers. Details of the possibilities may be obtained from the 'assessment' section of Priestley's book but a brief structure which is effective with social workers is as follows.

The material to be examined is divided into 'knowledge', 'feelings and attitudes' and 'skills'. This is a conventional educational division, but it may be difficult to apply in some cases. Making the distinctions in difficult cases can help to clarify many issues. Following this, means are devised of examining each of these areas in the past, present and future. For example checklists of agency tasks are given with scales against each one and this can show how much experience each team member has in each, and how much he would like. Open-ended exercises like sentence completion tests ("in social work practice, I like best . . ." or ". . . I like least"), can get at feelings and attitudes. Pattern notes help make links between apparently disparate subjects. Team members draw lines of different lengths showing areas of knowledge, the length of the line indicating the amount of knowledge, and connect up lines showing where they see connections between areas of knowledge. There are many other examples given by Priestley[11]. Although the suggestions here are for a general exercise, they can be adapted with a focus on part of the team's activities, for example, mental health, or social enquiry reports. These written exercises stimulate individual reflection about the issue in hand and are a personalised prelude to a process which builds up to involvement by the whole team. At the next stage the exercises are shared in pairs, so that individuals can test their responses with others in reasonable privacy. Because the material has been written down, differences in perception within each pair will be more evident and explicit. In normal team interaction, differences are often played down to avoid conflict and never explored and resolved. In pairs, team members can look at differences between the results of their exercises, and at things that stand out or surprise them in each other's exercises. They note issues arising from this which may affect other members of the team, and keep a record of personal needs for the future so that they can ensure that these are met somehow.

These points can now be brought to the whole team for group discussion. There may need to be an intermediate discussion in smaller groups if the group is very large. At the group discussion, the issues raised in smaller groups can be recorded, explored and questioned, and then priorities can be set. These stages might be divided into different structures in the programme – perhaps held at different sessions. Sometimes group exercises around some of these issues during the course of these sessions are helpful. Some exercises can be easily adapted from those suggested by Brandes and Phillips[12]. If a long session is planned, relaxation or warming up exercises from the same book can release tensions and break up the programme.

It will be seen, then, that such an exercise can focus attention on wide issues, or be limited to part of the team's responsibilities. It moves from and takes account of individual needs to the whole team's responsibilities. It is flexible and can be run in very truncated or very expanded form, over a long period or in a concentrated exercise. It is fun and stimulating, and with care team members can be protected if they need to move slowly in involvement in the team or in self-revelation in groups. Individuals can control how they respond to the written exercises and paired discussions and so limit the amount of self-revelation they are involved in to what is acceptable. This should be made clear and respected.

At the end of the exercise, several aspects of development discussed in the first part of this chapter should have been met. There should be better descriptions of the work of the team and individuals in it (including the team leader), there should be evaluations of that work and there should be sets of priorities and definitions of the requirements for future change.

Planning objectives

However the basic information is obtained the objectives which are to be achieved by any staff development activity need to be defined. Again, these may be divided into knowledge, skills and attitudes and feelings. Each individual needs development in all of these areas: so also may the team as a group.

Within the team, knowledge and skills may be present, but in the wrong person. For example, a team member may have experience of being a foster parent, but does not contribute to selecting and assessing foster parents. They may also be applied to one problem, but not to a slightly different problem to which they are transferable. Family therapy, for example, may be used where there are young children but not where elderly people are the focus of the problem. Feelings or attitudes which need change may exist in a team rather than individuals. For example, there may be a general view that working with the physically handicapped does not require a qualified social worker's skills, and this inhibits some who may wish to from doing this work. There is a common assumption that knowledge is valuable for itself. While this may be true in general, in a practical activity like social work, knowledge must be capable of application and this is particularly so in staff development which is concerned with the use of knowledge in fulfilling the agency's needs in actual practice. Skill has a rather similar problem: it is difficult to define it in ways which are capable of being put into operation. And it is difficult to operationalise any change in feelings and attitudes without seeming either presumptuous or dictatorial.

In planning objectives, therefore, it is useful to apply one of the principles identified in the first part of this chapter: that of deriving the objectives directly from practice. What was it, for example, that caused the chaos around Mrs. A's admission to hospital? It may be that the social worker's knowledge of her condition was poor, his skills in advocacy on her behalf inadequate, or his feeling of distaste for her handicap damaged his relationship with her. (It may also be organisational or policy issues unrelated to staff development). Using concrete examples of practice in this way and generalising from them (if appropriate) can identify clear issues for development in a more generalised way. Regular review of activities in cases for staff development objectives is an important responsibility of team leaders as they carry out supervision.

Having identified suitable needs and objectives, the various methods which might be used need to be evaluated.

Staff Supervision

The most obvious opportunity is that of personal supervision and consultation. A fuller examination of what is involved here is contained in two works by Kadushin[13] and the series of articles edited by Kaslow[14]. A number of general points may be made. First, it is important to distinguish between administrative supervision (designed to ensure that workers comply with agency requirements) and educational supervision (designed to aid their personal development as social workers). Failure to do so can cause great difficulty. Second a hierarchical relationship between worker and supervisor can cause difficulties but these are less likely to arise if the principle of working directly from cases is again used, and the evidence on which supervision is based is clear and unequivocal. It is also less likely to occur if the relationship is based on mutual respect for each other's abilities. Recent developments in supervising techniques, therefore, emphasise the visibility of individual's work to consultants and supervisors and vice versa. Supervisors and workers can be present at interviews together in various ways. One may go as an observer: not for the worker to be shown the 'better' supervisor at work, or for the supervisor to check up on the worker but so that they are both present when the evidence they will use in discussion is generated. Alternatively, one may go as a consultant, who can be referred to by the direct worker during the course of the interview or who can interrupt with advice as the interview proceeds. They can either agree to withdraw, or consult openly in front of clients. Another alternative is for both workers to take a role in the interview. For instance, in a family interaction, one worker could be mainly responsible for working with the parents in an interview while the other works to ensure the children are not left out.

With more sophisticated resources in the agency, additional techniques can be adopted. Where there are rooms with one-way mirrors, the consultant can see the interaction and be available to the worker, but not be too obtrusive in the interaction. Clients can also use the screen to see other members of their families or groups they are involved with, interacting without their presence. As well as, or instead of these facilities audio and video recordings of interviews can be used to base supervision sessions in the real interactions and help give workers feed-back about the responses to their interventions. Increasingly, many child and family guidance clinics and hospitals have these facilities available: they should be a daily part of the work of all agencies.

132

Using these techniques, feedback to the worker can be more immediate, based on a much fuller and checkable record of events in this work and directly oriented to work with clients. This means that workers have much more evidence, more quickly available, about their actual behaviour in social work relationships and can change and develop much more quickly than by using the more conventional longer-term methods of supervision based on discussion of often inadequate records well after the event.

Some supervisors in this situation find it difficult to allow the worker the freedom to have his own style. The tendency to intervene too much and too soon in 'live' supervision should be guarded against and Haley[16] gives a number of rules for supervisors which may help. In discussing details of social work in this way, it is easy to put others on the defensive, particularly if the supervisor is the worker's superior in a hierarchy, so it is useful to come to an agreement that what are pieces of advice and instructions will be clearly differentiated, and to offer comments which draw the worker's attention to events in his interviews, but not make explicit judgements about them before he has considered them.

It is also helpful if supervision works on objectives arrived at in the staff development programme, so that the general objectives in the team's programme are reflected in the detailed work carried out in supervision. Work which does not fall within those objectives can be dealt with by administrative supervision or consultation rather than the detailed coordination of skills and practice implied by educational supervision.

Training in the team

The second method of staff development is to seek resources within the team to contribute to training programmes. Many aspects of skill, knowledge and attitude development can be accomplished by more opportunities for practice. Sometimes this can be gained by the individual, given supervision, but it is often better achieved or only possible with others' help since this provides the confidence and stimulation to develop.

Structured opportunities can be provided in the team for members to pass on knowledge, skills and points of view which they have to others. A discussion group or teaching group may be one possibility but there are many others.

Visual aids, posters and checklists of information as assessment guidelines can all be offered by team members whose skills do not lie in leading discussions or giving information verbally. Group and individual projects to gain information not held within the team can also be fostered. Useful areas to look at are information about social work theories and practice, particular client groups, social problems faced by the team, resources available in other agencies, in the team's own agency, in the community and nationally, other professions and occupational groups and current political and social debates.

The development and practice of skills can be done in the team setting, by involving members of the team in shared work with peers like that described earlier in the section on supervision. Simulated experiences can be provided which staff can use to test out new skills before trying them with clients. The most commonly used simulations are case studies and role plays. Both these are better if there is a good deal of structure to guide what should be considered by the participants. More complicated simulations can be used to take people through a series of events or procedures and may construct a structure which responds like the environment, so that if participants make a wrong decision they learn about the unfortunate consequences. In devising simulations it is necessary to be clear about the learning objective and structure the elements accordingly. Two booklets published by the National Institute for Social Work[17] give details of games and exercises specifically designed for social services staff and Brandes and Phillips[18] give a wide range of games designed to stimulate learning about feelings and attitudes.

If discussion groups are used clear focus and objectives are helpful. As with all groups, some members may have to be protected from the aggressive or critical behaviour of others, particularly if it involves judgements about their work. Others may need to be drawn out by being given opportunities to offer their views on things about which the group leader is sure they will have a worthwhile contribution to make. In this way, their confidence to contribute may be enhanced in the future. Personal comments, even jokingly made, should be discouraged. The focus should be on practice rather than personality. It is important not to try to press people to speak if the leader thinks they are working quietly on a difficult matter for themselves, since this may prevent them from learning.

In all these situations, the team leader is attempting to expand experience and knowledge, while still retaining the worker's self-confidence. Where individuals have identified gaps in their knowledge or skill or unhelpful attitudes and feelings, it is useful to help them to retain confidence in their general ability or development activities may damage morale. A general air of confidence in individuals' work will go some way towards this. During supervision or other development activities it is also useful to help them extend themselves from a position of strength. In a new task, identifying factors which are similar to existing work in which they are confident and pointing out the links to existing knowledge and practice which is being developed can be helpful. Also, opportunities to rehearse or test out new activities through role plays, demonstrations or the opportunity to work with colleagues, can maintain confidence while new work is being approached. In addition, the careful management of work allocation can be used as part of staff development to expand practice knowledge and skill.

External resources

Not all the resources needed for staff development in the team are available within it, so the team leader is sometimes responsible for seeking additional resources from outside.

The first place to look is within the agency, particularly in training and development sections and in nearby agencies or the local community. Using others from within the agency may cement relationships which will be useful in other situations. If there is a local University, Polytechnic or College of Higher Education with a social work or social administration course, staff there may provide resources or advice on other people who could help. There is no need to be afraid of approaching people in these establishments; being asked for this kind of information is a normal part of the informal networks to which they belong and which they use in their work. Finally, people who have written articles or books about relevant subjects can be approached, and it is useful to keep a record of likely people so that it is easy to remember them. The staff of professional associations such as BASW and RCA or pressure groups such as MIND or Child Poverty Action Group may also be able to give advice about useful resources. Local people cost less to bring, are more likely to be in tune with local needs, and are less likely to charge a fee. Resources from outside the normal ambit of an agency on the other hand may bring a totally new approach which can be very stimulating.

As well as approaching individuals to help with something devised by the team, it is possible to approach organisations to provide standard courses in the team or agency. Pressure groups with training departments, like MIND or Age Concern, and local Universities may do so: perhaps approaches will have to be made through the agency's training section if there is one. On a grander scale, some organisations like the National Institute for Social Work can provide an extensive consultancy service. Social work, education, psychology and various medical departments in colleges may have something to offer.

Finally, it is possible to send team members on courses offered by various institutions and within the wider agency. They will have to be assessed by the team for relevance to their needs.

The guiding rule might be that these resources should only be used where they are necessary to fulfil needs first identified by the team and individuals. Areas where the team or an individual are unable to fulfil the basic responsibilities of the agency properly have top priority. Then topics which will enable the team to offer an improved quality or quantity of service which it is already providing. Topics where the objective is a new kind of service on top of a team's normal responsibilities come last. They should enhance the range of responses to community problems by the team or individuals.

These resources must also be coordinated into the team's programme. Some guiding principles here can be derived from Briggs[18] proposal, mentioned earlier, that inductive learning, from the particular to the general, is most appropriate in the first instance. Thus, the earliest efforts might be towards working within the team on the detail of responsibilities, describing and evaluating what is done more clearly. Then resources which aid the team in setting and working on new objectives might be the next priority with, at specific points outside resources tied into that where the team or individuals have clearly identified they are ready for taking on an already formulated approach and testing it out against what they perceive to be necessary for their work.

Finally, if resources are brought in from outside, particularly from a course with its own set of theoretical assumptions, careful preparations will be needed to ensure that the advantage is not lost. The team should be ready to take advantage of the additional resources obtained from the development. Other members of the team may have to be helped to understand how it will fit in to their work. Then, the new skill or knowledge should be reinforced and time and opportunities sought for its immediate and continuing practice, otherwise the impetus to do so will disappear. There should be a reward for the use of secured developments – not necessarily in promotion or more money, but in the team leader's recognition of progress being made explicit and the advantages to clients and the community being pointed out and stressed.

Promotion and formal reviews

One important aspect of staff development may be preparation for career progression in members of the team. Involvement in a valued staff development exercise within the team may provide the basis for a more formal structure of review. Whether that is the intention from the outset, or it arises after some project is underway, it should be made clear to the team and the issues of authority and power which are raised by the formal evaluation element of the programme dealt with explicitly within it. The evidence from the new approaches to supervision and the more effective evaluation of work in the team should make formal assessments of staff more acceptable. One danger which often arises is where problems are raised which have arisen in the past, but there is insufficient evidence of improvement to show that the worker has dealt with the problem, and there is resentment that old ashes are being raked over. Here, the model presented in the first part of this chapter may enable people in this situation to identify specific improvements which have taken place. Moving along the path from description to a secured development, a supervisor can see exactly how far a team member has progressed in developing out of a problem.

One objective staff may have is promotion, and the staff development activities outlined here are also relevant to that. The skills and experience needed for the particular move being proposed should be identified and staff ought to have opportunities to demonstrate that they have acquired them. For an appointment to a team leader's post, for example, social workers may need to show a greater ability to generalise about policy matters, to demonstrate their self-control and ability to provide structure, stimulation and motivation for others, and so on.

Comings and goings

Arrivals and departures in the team are not just important for the individuals concerned but for the losses and opportunities they make for the team. Integration and disengagement are major aspects of the staff development activities of the team and should be seen as natural parts of the life of any group.

If the team is committed to staff development, then development away from this team should be recognised as ultimate development for some. As developments are secured, further developments will eventually, though perhaps not immediately, need to be planned so that individuals do not stand still, and this may avoid the loss of a team member. If someone feels dissatisfied, therefore, it may be useful to look at what is not being fulfilled. This may be within himself: a skill, an area of knowledge or a feeling or attitude which is not being used or treated appropriately. Or it may be in the agency: an area of service, a client group, a method of working, a relationship with another profession which is not being exploited. From an examination of these issues, it may be possible to devise a staff development programme either for this individual or the team which meets the needs expressed. If leaving is the only course open for a member the team could examine explicitly what is being lost, how the loss can be met within the team or if it is necessary to devise a staff development programme to meet it. Such an explicit evaluation of the contribution of a team member can help him to leave, realising his value to the others, and help them to accept his leaving or, if they are inappropriately glad about it, realise for the first time what they are losing. Similarly as a team member arrives, a process of examining what he brings can help him to feel valued and to be making a contribution at an early stage. Such exercises around comings and goings also help other staff to realise the opportunities for development that such events offer them.

Comings and goings, then, illustrate the worth of staff development in the team. It values the individuals who serve the community in the team, and it enhances the value of the team itself as the instrument of that service.

References

1. Meyer, Carol H. *Staff Development in Public Welfare Agencies,* New York: Columbia University Press, 1966, p. 98.
2. Briggs, Thomas L. "In-service training for effective teamwork" in D. Brieland, T. Briggs and P. Leuenberger *The Team Model of Social Work Practice* New York: Syracuse University School of Social Work. Manpower Monograph No. 5, 1973, p. 35.
3. Pettes, Dorothy E. *Staff and Student Supervision: a task-centred approach* London: George Allen and Unwin, 1979, p. 61.
4. Thomas, David N. and Warburton, R. William, "Staff development in community work in social service departments" in C. Briscoe and D. N. Thomas (eds) *Community Work: Learning and Supervision,* London: George Allen and Unwin, 1977.
5. Cohen, Gertrude M. "Staff development in social work" in *Encylopaedia of Social Work,* 17th Issue Vol. 2, Washington: N.A.S.W., 1977.
6. Briggs, *ibid.*
7. Nixon, Stephen: Chapter in this volume.
8. Leydendecker, G. "A comprehensive staff development programme" *Social Casework* Vol. 46, No. 10, December 1965, pp. 607-613.
9. Payne, Malcolm and Dawson, Jenny "Student participation in social work education" *Social Work Today* Vol. 10, No. 20, pp. 24-26.
10. Priestley, P., McGuire, J., Flegg, D., Hemsley, V. and Welham, D. *Social Skills and Personal Problem Solving,* London: Tavistock Publications, 1978.
11. Priestley, *et al., op. cit.*
12. Brandes, Donna and Phillips, Howard, *Gamesters' Handbook* London: Hutchinson, 1979.
13. Kadushin, A. *Supervision in Social Work,* New York: Columbia University Press, 1976; *Consultation in Social Work,* New York: Columbia University Press, 1977.
14. Kaslow, F. W. and Associates: *Supervision, Consultation and Staff Training in the Helping Professions,* San Francisco: Jossey-Bass Publishers, 1977.
15. Haley, J. *Problem-solving Therapy,* San Francisco: Jossey-Bass Publishers, 1976, pp. 191-194.
16. MacDougall, Kay, *Simple Task-Centred Exercises* London: National Institute for Social Work Papers 4; McGaughan, N. and Scott, T., *Role play and Simulation Games: Uses in Social Work Education,* London: National Institute for Social Work Papers 9.
17. Brandes and Phillips, *op. cit.*
18. Briggs, *op. cit.* p. 35.